Considering Tomorrow
15 Changes to Prepare for

変わりゆく世界：明日の世界を考える15のトピック

by

James M. Vardaman

NOJI Kaoru

JN034081

TSURUMI SHOTEN

Considering Tomorrow:
15 Changes to Prepare for

Photo credits:

p. 1 © stoatphoto / PIXTA（ピクスタ）
p. 7 © Ystudio / PIXTA（ピクスタ）
p. 13 © Gesrey / PIXTA（ピクスタ）
p. 19 © show999 / PIXTA（ピクスタ）
p. 25 © metamorworks / PIXTA（ピクスタ）
p. 31 © JackF / PIXTA（ピクスタ）
p. 37 © luchschen / PIXTA（ピクスタ）
p. 43 © joykid / PIXTA（ピクスタ）
p. 49 © Fast&Slow / PIXTA（ピクスタ）
p. 55 © Kostiantyn Postumitenko / PIXTA（ピクスタ）
p. 67 © Graphs / PIXTA（ピクスタ）
p. 73 © takapon / PIXTA（ピクスタ）
p. 79 © kasto / PIXTA（ピクスタ）
p. 85 © YsPhoto / PIXTA（ピクスタ）

表紙／扉 © metamorworks / PIXTA（ピクスタ）

自習用音声について

本書の自習用音声は以下よりダウンロードできます。予習、復習にご利用ください。
（2022 年 4 月 1 日開始予定）

http://www.otowatsurumi.com/0053/

URL はブラウザのアドレスバーに直接入力して下さい。
パソコンでのご利用をお勧めします。圧縮ファイル (zip) ですのでスマートフォンでの場合は事前に解凍アプリをご用意下さい。

はしがき

　2019 年 12 月末に中国の武漢市で発生した新型コロナ肺炎の感染はその後世界中に拡大しました。コロナ禍は、各国の景気後退と市民の日常生活に大きな不自由をもたらし、世界各国で進んでいたグローバル化志向も、停滞を余儀なくされたようです。

　しかし、コロナ禍で人や物の国境を越えた移動が制限されても、IT は AI のとどまることを知らない進歩にも伴い、産業の現場だけでなく、好むと好まざるにかかわらず私たちの生活にもますます入り込んできています。科学の進歩とともに社会は、必ずしもプラスの面だけではないかもしれませんが、変わらざるを得ないのが現実です。それは今後の世界がコロナとの共生社会になるかどうかを問わず必然的に加速していくことでしょう。

　本書は IT による技術の革新が与える社会への影響、農業や漁業の変化、学習方法の変化、また人間生活に与える負の一面などのトピック、加えて大洋に浮遊するプラスティックの問題や化石燃料からのエネルギー転換問題など、現代科学がもたらした負の遺産についての問題なども含め、きょうの世界を知り明日の社会を考える 15 のトピックを集めました。

　そして、ここに収めた 15 のトピックはバラエティに富んでいるので、理系文系を問わずにどのクラスでも興味を持って読んで貰えることと確信しています。

　加えて、本書には英文それ自体がきちんと読めているかどうかをチェックする設問が本文の随所に設けられています。また、文法問題とリスニング問題も各章ごとにつけて総合的な英語力がつくように配慮してあります。さらに、学生のみなさんが物事を自分の頭で考え、自分の意見を自分の言葉で表すことの一助になるように各章末にディスカッションや自習用の設問を付けてあります。

　本書が学生の皆さんの英語力の向上とともに社会の現実と進化をよく知りよく考える一助となってくれることを願っています。

2021 年 11 月

James M. Vardaman

Contents

CHAPTER 1

Universal Basic Income

　完璧な世界があるとすれば、そこでは職業は自由に選択でき、そこそこの収入が得られて快適な生活が過ごせることだろう。自分の選ぶ道に進むために必要な教育や訓練も受けられるし、将来についても見通しを立てやすい。

　しかし、現実は甘くない。会社の浮沈に憂き目を見るかもしれないし、技術革新の波のあおりを受けて、家族ともども経済的苦境に陥ることもあるだろう。

　そんな時に必要なのが政府による支援だ。世界ではどんな考え方のもとで、どんなことが行われているのだろうか……。

Universal Basic Income

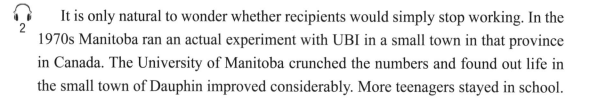

In a perfect world, people would be able to find a job that they enjoy and be paid a wage that allows them to live comfortably. They would have financial support to get a good education and training for that job. They could be assured that their job would continue for the foreseeable future. Our world, however, is not perfect. Companies can close or move elsewhere. Skills that were once sufficient grow outdated. To support a ⁵ family and avoid poverty during difficult times, it becomes necessary to get help from the government in the form of welfare assistance. But some people are now promoting another alternative: Universal Basic Income.

The idea behind Universal Basic Income (UBI) is to eliminate poverty, immediately. By providing a financial cushion to those who are temporarily out of work, those who ¹⁰ are working only part-time, those who are going to school, or those being retrained for new jobs, a monthly UBI payment would be a great help.

● NOTES ●

4 **for the foreseeable future**「ここ当分の間は」／9 **Universal Basic Income (UBI)**「ベーシックインカム」
政府が全ての国民に対し所得保障として一定の現金を定期的に支給する制度。／10 **are temporarily out of work**「一時的に失業中の」

✳ *Comprehension Check* ✳

1. Which of the following statements is true?
   a. The skills we have will always be useful.
   b. Sometimes the government has to help people avoid poverty.
   c. Everyone can get a good education.

2. Who would Universal Basic Income be given to?
   a. People who are not working full time.
   b. Families with several children.
   c. Children living away from their parents.

It is only natural to wonder whether recipients would simply stop working. In the 1970s Manitoba ran an actual experiment with UBI in a small town in that province in Canada. The University of Manitoba crunched the numbers and found out life in the small town of Dauphin improved considerably. More teenagers stayed in school.

Hospitalization rates decreased. Work rates remained basically stable. The program 5
worked quite well.

Economists and policy strategists are looking at the Dauphin experiment again. With employers relocating, jobs moving offshore, traditional blue-collar jobs decreasing, automation expanding, and education costs rising, the idea of a basic income guarantee is increasingly seen as a means of preventing people from falling 10 below the poverty line. To leftists, it is seen as a way of combatting the income gap and freeing workers from the burden of taking dead-end jobs. To conservatives, it seems like a better alternative to social-welfare and anti-poverty programs. It would be simple to administer—reducing government bureaucracy—and it would be provided to everyone. 15

●NOTES●

2 **Manitoba**「マニトバ州」カナダ中部にある州。／3 **crunched the numbers**「（答えを見つけるために）データを大量に処理した」／4 **Dauphin**「ドーフィン」マニトバ州にある町。1974–79 年にベーシックインカム導入に向けた社会実験を実施した。2011 年にその成果をまとめた報告書がマニトバ大学から発表された。／5 **hospitalization rates**「入院加療率」／11 **the poverty line**「貧困ライン」最低限度の生活を送るのに必要な所得水準。／12 **dead-end jobs**「将来性のない仕事」／14 **administer**「（行政的に）処理する」／14 **government bureaucracy**「政府官僚」

✳ *Comprehension Check* ✳

3. What did the experiment in Manitoba find out?
   a. Life in Dauphin worked rather well.
   b. Local jobs decreased.
   c. More people went to the hospitals.

4. Which of the following is NOT true about Universal Basic Income?
   a. Leftists and conservatives find it attractive.
   b. Automation is one cause of an increase in poverty.
   c. The program would be available only to students and blue-collar workers.

Workers could take short breaks to study, upgrade their skills, or even take care of children or elderly relatives. Single parents would be able to support their families with part-time work, rather than have to choose between full-time jobs and being at home with their young children. Most importantly, recipients would not have to worry about covering monthly bills. It would give them the basic security of knowing 5 that if they work, they will not live in poverty.

In January 2017 Finland began paying a random sample of 2,000 unemployed people aged 25 to 58 a monthly 560 Euros. The recipients were under no obligation to seek or accept employment during the two-year trial. Anyone who took a job would continue to receive the same amount. In the growing "gig economy," it offered financial security to those whose incomes are variable. 10

While some worry that the UBI scheme simply gives money to citizens for nothing, others compare it to investing in infrastructure. It creates a "new road" that allows people to be more productive. It provides freedom and flexibility to do what one wants, even if it doesn't pay particularly well. It provides a safety net for those 15 who want to change jobs. A small percent of recipients may choose to do nothing at all, but the trial in Finland may provide lessons for the future of welfare around the globe.

● NOTES ●

7 **a random sample** 「無作為に抽出された標本 (母集団)」／9 **during the two-year trial**「2年の試験期間中」／10 **gig economy**「ギグエコノミー」インターネットを通じて単発や短期間の仕事を請け負う働き方やそれによって成り立つ経済形態をいう。／15 **a safety net**「安全保証、頼みの綱」

✱ Comprehension Check ✱

5. What happened in the Finland experiment?
   a. Recipients paid back the money after two years.
   b. People could receive the money and take a job too.
   c. The young recipients went back to school.

❁ Structure Practice ❁

A. Choose the one underlined word or phrase that should be corrected or rewritten. Then change it so the sentence is correct.

1. With a university ₁degree, many people would be ₂insured that they would have a ₃secure job that would last a ₄lifetime. [   ]

2. Without government ₁support, it is difficult to ₂guarantee that families with only ₃part-time jobs and a family to take care of can ₄prevent falling into poverty. [   ]

B. Choose the word or phrase that best completes the sentence.

3. When we refer to jobs moving offshore we mean that . . .
   a. employees go abroad.   b. workers in other countries take the job.
   c. products are sold overseas.   d. jobs are done by machines.

4. Dead-end jobs do not . . . to further developments of skills.
   a. evolve   b. guide   c. lead   d. move

5. If you are . . . new ideas and up-to-date information, online learning is certainly one good option.
   a. attracting   b. looking   c. seeking   d. upgrading

❁ Listening Challenge ❁

🎧 **Listen and fill in the missing words.**

4

1. There was a time when it [   ] studying hard and getting a university education because that would [   ] to find a good job after graduation and [   ] the same company until retirement.

2. The governments of various countries are [   ] some form of basic income, whether it be provided [   ], even people with regular jobs, or [   ] without full-time employment.

3. The Manitoba experiment [   ] there are definite advantages to UBI [   ] work stability, health, and [   ] schools.

4. When companies relocate, local employees [   ] to either find new jobs in the same town or [   ] another place where there are more jobs to [   ].

5. I'm trying to [   ] my skills by taking online courses and [   ] special training courses [   ] and during my vacations.

Going Further (for discussion or research)

1. Would a Basic Income be a good idea for Japan?

2. As a fundamental idea, should everyone get such an income, even if they have a full-time job?

CHAPTER 2

Farms without Land

　農業に新しい世代の若者たちが革新をもたらしている。なんと、耕作地や、トラクターなどの機器を必要としないどころか、土壌、日光にも頼らないというものだ。

　日光を必要としないキノコ作りや、水栽培による小規模な植物育成などは従来から行われてきた。しかし画期的な発想の転換をもたらしたのはLEDの発明だ。建物の中で比較的安価に、ハイテクを駆使して「擬似」自然環境を作り出せるようになったからだ。

　ニューヨークなどの大都市のど真ん中に高層ビルの農場を作ろうというアイデアもあるようだ。たしかに気候変動や害虫、雑草も管理可能で、究極の地産地消かもだが……。

Farms without Land

A new generation of farmers is breaking with tradition. They have no fields, no tractors or harvesters, and no barn. In fact, they have no soil and some don't even have sunlight.

In the cloudy city of Seattle, Dan Albert grows his crops in his farm which is located in his two-car garage. He produces tiny green plants called microgreens, 5 which include radishes and arugula, popular ingredients in salads. Instead of fields covered with soil, he grows them in vertically stacked trays that slowly rotate. Instead of sunlight, he depends on LED lights. In the limited space within his garage, he grows them with hydroponics, a system that allows the plant's roots to sit in nutrient-rich water, instead of in soil. Within two weeks his crops go from seed to harvest to 10 restaurants, farmers' markets, and local groceries. His microgreens are competitive in price with major farms and they are fresh.

The shift away from soil-based farming is not limited to spare garages and bedrooms. The shift is not limited to ground level either. New farmers are making use of tall, multi-floor former factories and empty warehouses, making "vertical farming" 15 a new way to produce food.

● NOTES ●

6 **arugula**「ルッコラ」／ 7 **virtually stacked trays**「垂直に積み重ねられたトレイ」／ 9 **with hydroponics**「水耕栽培で」／ 13 **soil-based farming**「土壌ベースの農業」／ 15 **vertical farming**「垂直農法」

✳ *Comprehension Check* ✳

1. According to the article, traditional farming has depended on . . .
   a. fields, sunlight, and machinery.
   b. growing many crops in the same farm.
   c. rapid transportation of large crops to markets.

2. Dan Albert's method does NOT use . . .
   a. seeds or soil.
   b. water or farm land.
   c. soil or sunlight.

🎧
6 Admittedly, these larger-scale enterprises require more equipment, water, and electricity for the LEDs that mimic sunlight. Control software, however, can ensure that the rotating racks of plants get the same amount of light, and the pumps distribute an even amount of nutrients. Sensors discover which crops flourish with different wavelengths of light and adjust the lighting accordingly. Since these "farms" are 5 indoors, the systems can be run on off-peak energy, for example, between 7:00 p.m. and 7:00 a.m., when electricity rates are lower.

In Singapore, which has a very low food self-sufficiency rate and a burgeoning population, a public-private enterprise is taking hydroponics seriously. Electricity for LEDs and tray rotation motors can be expensive in large-scale operations. The Sky 10 Greens vertical farm, however, takes advantage of Singapore's sunny weather. The four-story glass-sided farm requires no artificial lighting at all. Racks of vegetables rotate up to the sunny top of the building on a power-efficient elevator, giving each rack a dose of light.

●NOTES●

3 **the rotating racks**「回転するラック」／5 **wavelengths**「波長」／6 **can be run**「作動できる」／8 **food self-sufficiency rate**「食料自給率」／8 **burgeoning**「増大する」／13 **power efficient**「電力効率の良い、省電力」／14 **a dose of**「一定量の」

✷ *Comprehension Check* ✷

3. "Vertical farming" can be controlled by software that . . .
   a. guarantees that all plants get the same nutrient-rich water.
   b. eliminates insects and dryness.
   c. uses expensive electricity.

4. Which statement is true of the Sky Green vertical farm?
   a. Plants are placed in racks that do not move.
   b. Farmers use an elevator to reach the top trays.
   c. It does not depend on electricity to provide light.

🎧
7 As a result of considerable success with these nine-meter tall towers in Singapore, one ecologist has imagined an even greater vertical farm. His idea is to build a 21-story transparent skyscraper in the heart of a major city such as New York. His plan would

grow the produce in the middle of the market where it would be consumed. With
a very small footprint on the ground level, a large amount of food could be grown 5
inside the community that would consume it.

High-tech agribusiness has several important impacts. One is the reduced need
for pesticides and herbicides. It is much easier to prevent damage to crops inside
a building than in an open field. Second is the savings in fuel required to transport
harvested crops to markets if the vertical farm is in the city. Third is the protection of 10
food supplies even when extreme weather strikes. A final advantage is that software
can handle much of the day-to-day tending of the crops. The farmer can check on
several farms remotely, adjusting water, tray rotation speed, and mechanical problems
with a smartphone.

● NOTES ●
5 **footprint**「敷地面積」／8 **pesticides and herbicides**「殺虫剤と除草剤」 -cide「…を殺す薬剤」／11
extreme weather「異常気象」／12 **day-to-day**「毎日の」

✱ *Comprehension Check* ✱

5. Which statement is true of high-tech indoor farming?
    a. It does not require any human activity.
    b. It avoids weather damage caused by growing crops in open fields.
    c. It does not require any light.

❈ Structure Practice ❈

A. Choose the one underlined word or phrase that should be corrected or rewritten. Then change it so the sentence is correct.

1. In traditional ₁<u>farming</u>, the crops that a farmer can grow ₂<u>dependent</u> on the quality of the soil, ₃<u>the average</u> temperatures, weather, and ₄<u>availability of</u> markets.

   [   ]

2. Global warming has a strong ₁<u>impact</u> what crops we can grow, ₂<u>whether there</u> is ₃<u>enough water</u> for them, and what kind of insects ₄<u>might destroy</u> them.

   [   ]

B. Choose the word or phrase that best completes the sentence.

3. If something is transparent, . . .
   a. we are unable to see it.   b. it is invisible.
   c. we are able to see through it.   d. it can't be seen.

4. Corn . . . a significant portion of the feed given to cattle.
   a. composes   b. compounds   c. comprises   d. consists

5. Rainforests . . . because of the rain and heat.
   a. advance   b. bear fruit   c. flourish   d. multiply

❈ Listening Challenge ❈

🎧 **Listen and fill in the missing words.**
8

1. As [   ] the new dam on the Nile River in Ethiopia, Ethiopia, Egypt, and [   ] countries are currently [   ] over water rights.

2. On large farms, by [   ], farmers can [   ] their crops without spending large [   ] time.

3. The [   ] a farm is to the market where its [   ], the fresher the product and the cheaper [   ].

4. Tractors and [   ] can be expensive to purchase and [   ], so some farmers cooperate [   ] in buying and sharing them.

5. Farming is a [   ] business, which is [   ] by weather, markets, and [   ] variables.

Going Further (for discussion or research)

1. Would vertical farms be practical in urban areas in Japan?

2. What edible plants could you grow at home?

3. How do you view the future of farming in Japan?

CHAPTER 3

Facial Recognition

何の手続きをするにも、やれ免許証だのパスポートだのマイナンバーカードだの主に顔写真付きのものが、本人である証明としてはまだ主流である。

　各種イベントなどで利用される「顔認証」システムは、発展途上ではある。性別や人種の判別を誤るということもあるらしい。また、誰もがこのシステムの使用に同意するわけではなく、ネット上の画像を無断で使用したと裁判沙汰になることもある。

　防犯カメラが歩行者の信号無視を捉え、瞬時に、交差点のスクリーンに本人の個人情報がさらけ出された様子が公開されたことがあった。中国の話だが……。

Facial Recognition

🎧
9

Not long ago, it was necessary to present an ID with a photograph to prove who you are. Whether it was on a driver's license, a credit card, or a passport, a photo was supposed to be evidence that connected you to your name, gender, age, and address. This photo was essential if you wanted to drive a car, charge a purchase, or prove that you were the legal age to buy alcohol. Today, we are rapidly entering an age in which ₅ a photo ID is no longer necessary. People already know a lot about us without seeing our ID card.

Fans attending sports events have long gone through metal detectors and bag searches. The new additions are the cameras that scan the faces of people as they pass through the gates. These images are immediately processed by facial-recognition ₁₀ software which is supposed to identify people who might present a security risk. Facial recognition, however, is not perfect. For example, it misidentifies women and African Americans more frequently than white men, according to a researcher at the M.I.T. Media Lab. If it misidentifies people, then it cannot completely guarantee security either.

₁₅

●NOTES●

2– **was supposed to be**「～であるはずだった」／4 **charge a purchase**「クレジットカードで買い物をする」／8 **metal detectors**「金属探知機」／11 **might present a security risk**「危険人物になりかねない」／14 **M.I.T.**「マサチューセッツ工科大学」*M*assachusetts *I*nstitute of *T*echnology

✱ *Comprehension Check* ✱

1. Which statement is NOT true?
    a. A photo ID has only been necessary for driving a car.
    b. A passport has been one form of photo ID.
    c. A credit card without a photo is accepted as an ID.

2. Facial-recognition software . . .
    a. has not been perfect in identifying certain types of people.
    b. has completely replaced photo IDs.
    c. is banned at many sports events.

🎧 10   Facial recognition software seems harmless enough. A few American churches use it to help them track the attendance of worshippers on Sunday morning. It is making inroads in ordinary stores, too. It scans the faces of shoppers, identifying returning customers who might be offered special prices on items in the store.

    But not everyone is pleased about the use of facial recognition without permission. 5 In the U.S., for example, lawsuits have been filed against Facebook, claiming that their "faceprints" have been taken and used without their "informed written consent." When a user of Facebook, for example, appears in a photograph, the person can be "tagged" if he or she appears in a photo uploaded by a friend. The user may not even realize that the photo is on the Internet, with his or her name attached. What is 10 even creepier is that anyone with a phone can take a picture for a facial-recognition program to use.

●NOTES●

2 **the attendance of worshippers**「礼拝に出席した人たち」／3 **making inroads in**「～に入り込む」／6 **lawsuits have been filed against**「～に対して訴訟が起こされている」／10 **What is even creepier**「さらに ぞっとすること」

✽ Comprehension Check ✽

3. Identifying a person's face and tagging it on the internet with his or her name . . .
    a. is not something everyone likes.
    b. has no negative effect.
    c. is not allowed by law.

🎧 11   Privacy in public is under threat in many other countries as well. Law enforcement agencies are already analyzing "facial geometry" by cameras in public spaces, at street corners, in subways, and over highways. In China, for example, a facial-recognition surveillance system captures pedestrians caught jaywalking. It then displays their photo—together with their name and social identification numbers—on LED screens 5 at road junctions. There are 170 million CCTV cameras in the country already, not just watching, but analyzing data in real time and showing it to the public.

    As facial technology improves, it can have unexpected results. Researchers at Stanford University, for example, have demonstrated that one app can attribute a person's sexuality correctly 81% of the time, 20% better than humans can do. In 10 countries where homosexuality is a crime, an app that infers sexual orientation from a photo of a face is frightening to consider. In less harsh countries, facial recognition programs could make bias a routine occurrence. It could allow companies to filter all job applicants by signs of genetic conditions, intelligence, sexuality, and ethnicity.

● NOTES ●

1 **Law enforcement agencies**「法執行機関、警察機関」／2 **facial geometry**「顔の幾何学的配置」／3 **facial-recognition surveillance system**「顔認証監視システム」／4 **jaywalking**「信号を無視して道路を横断すること」／6 **CCTV camera**「防犯カメラ」CCTV は *Closed Circuit Television*「閉回路テレビ」のことで、特定の建物や施設内での有線のテレビ。／10 **~ of the time**「～の割合で」／11 **sexual orientation**「(同性・異性・両性愛志向などの) 性愛的志向」

✳ *Comprehension Check* ✳

4. Privacy in public is . . .

   a. protected by "facial geometry."

   b. threatened by analysis data from facial-recognition surveillance.

   c. is a basic human right.

5. Facial-recognition technology . . .

   a. does not distinguish genders.

   b. enables police to find missing persons.

   c. can be used in bias in job applications.

❊ Structure Practice ❊

A. Choose the one underlined word or phrase that should be corrected or rewritten. Then change it so the sentence is correct.

1. When ₁searching for information on a search engine on the internet it is difficult to ₂determine what is ₃accuracy and what is not, so we must be ₄cautious.

    [   ]

2. Whether or not you are ₁awareness of it, there is a ₂considerable amount of information about you and your activities being ₃monitored by surveillance cameras in ₄public places.

    [   ]

B. Choose the word that best completes the sentence.

3. A good friend from high school waved at me from a long distance, but I didn't . . . him because he was wearing a big hat and a mask.

    a. identify   b. notify   c. realize   d. recognize

4. I received a photo from a friend with a note . . . saying that he had taken it during his vacation in Hawaii.

    a. attached   b. inserted   c. positioned   d. taped

5. The job application form included the . . . questions about previous employment, experience, and skills.

    a. appropriate   b. attribute   c. identified   d. routine

❊ Listening Challenge ❊

🎧 **Listen and fill in the missing words.**
12

1. Liquor stores in America are very [   ] checking photo IDs of customers, because [   ] are strict and they might lose their license to sell liquor [   ].

2. We were [   ] return by six o'clock, but our first train [
        ], we missed our connection, and there wasn't another train [
        ].

3. [   ] the newspapers, [   ] at the rally was significantly
    larger than anticipated, so the sponsors [   ] pleased.

4. The city government [   ] a lawsuit against the company for [
        ] complete the construction of the new street by the [   ]
    deadline.

5. The ability [   ] data in real time can make delivery of [   ]
    much more efficient and [   ] as well.

Going Further (for discussion or research)

1. Is it possible to hide your identity in public places? How could you do it?

2. What are the benefits and disadvantages of social platforms like Facebook?

CHAPTER 4

Automated Transportation

　前世紀には車の発明で人々は「自立」の恩恵に浴した。今はどうか。歩行者、自転車族は常にスピードを出す車の危険にさらされている。信号待ちや穴ポコ道での徐行、各種工事による渋滞は日常茶飯事で、ドライバーのストレスもたまったものではない。

　配車サービスなどを利用すれば、コストは自家用車の半分で済むという試算もある。また、各メーカーがこぞって開発を進めている自動運転システムと連動させれば、安全面と諸経費節減にも資する。自動運転システムは現状ではまだ課題は多いが、実用化するのはそんな先の話ではないだろう……。

Automated Transportation

13   In the twentieth century, cars gave us independence, but they also brought us new problems. Today pedestrians and bicyclists deal with speeding vehicles and drivers deal with traffic signals, potholes, bumper-to-bumper traffic, and road construction during their commutes and trips to the shopping areas, enduring stress and frustration.

And most cars aren't even on the road. It is estimated that the average car is   5 only used 5% of the time. During the other 95%, the car occupies space in a garage or a parking lot, both of which cost money and take up space. But in places where public transportation is inconvenient or even non-existent, the car has seemed like a necessity. Then around 2015, ride-hailing services such as Uber and Lyft began to change how people perceive private transportation.   10

In that year, people began to sense that actually owning a car might not be essential. Admittedly, a ride-hailing service in most wealthy countries is estimated to cost about double per kilometer what it costs to own and operate a private car. But if a person can call a ride, get picked up quickly, pay with a smartphone, and reach a destination easily, ride-hailing is appealing. Having taken that step forward in the   15 perception of transportation, people are going one step further. Is having a driver really essential?

●NOTES●
2 **speeding vehicles**「スピード違反の車」／3 **bumper-to-bumper traffic**「交通渋滞」／7 **take up space** 「場所をとる」／9 **ride-hailing services**「配車サービス」／9 **Uber**　アメリカの Uber Technologies Inc. が 運営するオンライン配車サービス／9 **Lyft**　サンフランシスコで 2012 年に開始されたライドシェア型のオンライン 配車サービス。

✳ *Comprehension Check* ✳

1. Which statement is NOT true?
   a. Automobiles created a mixture of conveniences and problems.
   b. Automobiles spend most of the time in motion.
   c. Public transportation isn't available everywhere.

2. Ride-hailing services . . .
   a. cost more per kilometer than owning a private car.
   b. have proven to be difficult to use.
   c. will replace car ownership in the next decade.

14
Wouldn't it be great if the technological revolution we are experiencing came up with an autonomous vehicle (AV), cars that can drive themselves? After all, 60% of the cost of a ride goes to paying the driver. If there is no driver, then transportation could cost less than half of the current rate. Seeing a paradigm shift in the making, established automobile manufacturers, tech companies and startups have begun ₅ testing the waters.

Eliminating the driver is not easy. Computers, sensors, cameras, and industrial designers are doing an increasingly better job at creating the vehicles, but they have not been able to replace the human operator completely. Furthermore, there is resistance from potential riders. Surveys show that most people would be unwilling ₁₀ to ride in a self-driving vehicle due to lack of trust or fear of giving up control to a machine.

●NOTES●
2 **autonomous vehicle (AV)**「自動運転車」／4 **paradigm shift**「パラダイムシフト」ものの見方を根本的に規定している概念を変えること。／5– **startups have begun testing the waters**「新興企業は水を試すことを始めている」水を燃料にして水素ガスで走る車の実験ことを言っている。startup「新興企業；ベンチャー企業」10 **potential riders**「乗り手となりうる人たち」

✳ *Comprehension Check* ✳

3. Without a driver, an autonomous vehicle would be . . .
    a. available to everyone.
    b. easy to use in any city.
    c. less expensive to use.

4. Many potential riders . . .
    a. are not willing to ride in an autonomous vehicle.
    b. trust technology to make AVs safe.
    c. will use AV cars without worrying.

15
Because human error is responsible for a high percentage of traffic accidents, one could argue that AVs would actually reduce road deaths. Tests with driverless vehicles on off-road courses have been carried out since 2004, beginning with mixed results. As safety has improved rapidly, various research groups—both government and private—have begun trials on public roads. ₅

Concerns about cyber-security, liability, and safety are side-effects raised by AV development. More significant issues are how to get the combination of cameras, radar and radar-like LIDAR to identify rarely seen items such as debris, plastic bags blowing across the road, puddles of water, and snow in the air. All of these are challenges that a human driver usually learns to handle.　　　　　　　　　　　10

The potential advantages of AV transportation ensure that governments, companies, and tech experts will continue efforts to solve the problems. Whether the public will embrace driverless vehicles will depend on the elimination of risks and whether AVs create more problems that we have not yet imagined. We will not need to wait until the next century to find out.　　　　　　　　　　　15

●NOTES●
1 **is responsible for**「～の原因となる」／ 2 **road deaths**「交通事故死亡者数」／ 6 **side-effects**「副産物」／ 8 **LIDAR**「ライダー（レーザーレーダー）」レーダーと同じ原理で物体を検出し場所を特定する測定システム、レーザーからの光を利用する。／ 8 **debris**「破片」／ 9 **puddles of water**「水たまり」

✳ *Comprehension Check* ✳

5. The appeal of AV transportation . . .
    a. is that it can do everything a human driver can.
    b. will improve roads and bridges.
    c. keeps companies and governments active in finding solutions to problems.

❊ Structure Practice ❊

A. Choose the one underlined word or phrase that should be corrected or rewritten. Then change it so the sentence is correct.

1. When they are not ₁in use, vehicles ₂take out a ₃lot of space in parking lots in public areas and ₄in places of employment.   [   ]

2. Advancing technology ₁is taking steps ₂toward promoting autonomous cars, ₃eliminate of drivers, and reducing ₄traffic accidents.   [   ]

B. Choose the word or phrase that best completes the sentence.

3. A high percentage of road accidents is . . . human error, so AVs would be a step forward in promoting safety.
   a. carried out   b. due to   c. operated   d. responsible

4. In isolated areas drones are able to . . . road vehicles as means of delivering emergency medicine during disasters.
   a. change   b. exchange   c. replace   d. substitute

5. Well-known businesses are currently involved in carrying . . . rocket flights with civilian passengers.
   a. about   b. out   c. over   d. through

❊ Listening Challenge ❊

🎧 **Listen and fill in the missing words.**
16
1. At the turn of the twentieth [   ], transportation and [
            ] in New York City and other [   ] were dependent on horses [   ] the streets dirty and unhealthy.

2. At one time, [   ] an automobile was [   ] dream that was hard to [   ] because they were too expensive for [   ] worker.

3. In America, pickup trucks are [   ] among people in small towns and in the [   ] because they not only haul [   ] but also transport [   ] in rugged terrain.

4. For some reason [   ] riding in a vehicle on a road [   ] operator or driver leaves most people [   ], although they feel comfortable in [   ] vehicles on tracks.

5. One can't help [   ] how a group of [   ] would be willing to [   ] near-Earth space in a rocket without [   ] on board.

Going Further (for discussion or research)

1. What is your perspective on the future of autonomous vehicles (AV)?

2. Why does the younger generation of Japanese feel it is not important to own a car?

CHAPTER *5*

Machine Learning

　「機械学習」に画期的な変化をもたらしたのが「ビッグデータ」と呼ばれるものだ。今や新たなツールとしてビジネス、行政、教育など各方面で活用されている。

　授業の形態も変化するかもしれない。機械が個人のレベルを判断し、緻密なプログラムで個別に指導するのも可能になるという。当然だが、これには反論もある。

　そこで AI が強みを持つデータベースの認識、分類、予測能力と、人間の洞察力を融合させた「人間参加型 AI」と呼ばれる機械学習モデルが開発されているのだが、人間が補正を加える嗜好を認識した AI が、さらにその先を行くなんてことになりはしないか……。

Machine Learning

17

The revolution in machine learning employing what we now call Big Data provides several new "tools" for business, government, and education. It supplies new sources of information; it captures what people actually do and think, rather than what they say they do and think; it allows researchers, hospitals, schools, and businesses to focus on demographic or social groups; and it can help find not just   5
correlation but also causality. It not only tells us what, but also tells us how and why.

Businesses have long used information technology to find out where their goods and services are selling. Now with Big Data, however, they can also predict where those goods and services might sell, too. Some companies are already using machine learning to filter through job applications, flagging candidates positively   10
or negatively based on their hobbies, names, and skills. Credit card companies use automated processes to quickly detect credit card fraud. Headquarters of convenience store holding companies can plot out potential sites for building a new store.

●NOTES●
 1 **Big Data** 従来のデータベース管理システムなどでは対処できない莫大で複雑で複雑なデータ群。／5
demographic「人口統計の」／6 **correlation**「相関関係」／6 **causality**「因果関係」／10 **flagging**「フラグつけて目印にする」／12 **credit card fraud**「クレジットカード詐欺」／12 **Headquarters**「本部；本社」
単数・複数扱い。／13 **potential site**「有望な場所」

�֍*Comprehension Check*�֍

1. Big Data supplies information based on . . .
   a. the opinions of large groups of people.
   b. what people actually do.
   c. people's age and gender.

2. A new use of Big Data is . . .
   a. evaluating people applying for jobs.
   b. finding good hobbies to recommend.
   c. locating schools in new neighborhoods.

In medicine, medical schools and hospitals train doctors to predict heart attacks so that they can take action before an attack occurs. Skilled physicians using manual systems, published research, and years of experience correctly predict around 30% of these events. A talking robot using a machine-learning application with historic data has been created that raises that figure to 80%, a significant advance. In some 5 hospitals, medical diagnosis of skin cancer from images—using results from previous images and subsequent biopsies—is already producing higher accuracy than human doctors.

Machine learning is playing an increasingly important role in education, from elementary school through university. Arizona State University is already 10 experimenting with machine learning, in part as a money-saving measure. Freshman volunteers have been learning math with a computer as the instructor. There is a professor in the room, but he or she doesn't lecture. The professor instead moves about the room coaching students when they get stuck on a particular problem. The professor can see immediately how each student is progressing and does not need to 15 grade the students. The computer software does the grading.

●NOTES●

4 **these events** 心臓発作のこと／6 **medical diagnosis**「医療診断」／7 **biopsies** ＜ biopsy「生体組織検査」／14 **get stuck**「行き詰まる」

✽ *Comprehension Check* ✽

3. In the medical field, machine-learning with Big Data . . .

    a. correctly predicted heart attacks at least 30 percent of the time.

    b. has been more successful than doctors in predicting heart attacks.

    c. is less accurate than doctors in predicting illnesses.

4. Arizona State University has begun experimenting with . . .

    a. eliminating professors from the classroom.

    b. evaluating teachers by using machine learning.

    c. machine learning teamed with a professor in the classroom.

🎧 19   The advantage in the classroom is that the students can go at their own pace, with faster learners learning on their own, while slower learners can get more help in learning a mathematical concept. The software uses billions of data points to determine what works well for a particular type of student and adjusts the material accordingly. By adapting questions to each student's ability, some schools claim, 5 every student receives individualized instruction at an affordable cost. Critics say that such data-driven "adaptive learning" threatens to turn schools into factories. Instead of putting computers in front of students, they say, schools should spend more on training and encouraging good teachers.

   In almost every field in which future automation is predicted, "machine learning" 10 will require what some call "a learning apprentice," or "the human in the loop." The human expert is not replaced but is assisted by artificial intelligence. Obviously, this shift will require that humans adapt to new ways of thinking—for all of the humans involved in any of the transactions mentioned above. And there is little doubt that the machines will adapt, too—just faster.   15

●NOTES●
   7 **data-driven**「データ主導の」／ 11 **a learning apprentice**「技能見習い者」／ 11 **the human in the loop** 人工知能などによって自動化・自律化が進んだ機械やシステムにおいて、一部の判断や制御にあえて人間を介在させること。略称 HITL。／ 14 **transactions**「トランザクション」IT 用語で複数の処理を一つにまとめたもの。

✳ *Comprehension Check* ✳

5. In the years to come, "machine learning" will . . .
   a. probably be used together with a human expert.
   b. replace human experts to a large degree.
   c. be used to assist slow learners master mathematics.

❊ Structure Practice ❊

A. Choose the one underlined word or phrase that should be corrected or rewritten. Then change it so the sentence is correct.

1. On the ₁basis of evidence that ₂is currently available we can't ₃help to view his behavior ₄negatively.   [   ]

2. By ₁employment machine learning in classrooms, universities ₂enable students to learn certain skills at their ₃own pace and allow instructors to focus on assisting students who need ₄personal assistance.   [   ]

B. Choose the word that best completes the sentence.

3. The introduction of Big Data in medical diagnosis will . . . doctors to act sooner to prevent heart attacks.
   a. allow   b. apply   c. promote   d. require

4. When businesses consider hiring new employees, they read . . . large numbers of applications before determining which applicants to call in for interviews.
   a. about   b. into   c. out   d. through

5. During my daily walk, I bumped into someone I had met before, but I was lost . . . where we had met the first time.
   a. about   b. by   c. on   d. over

❊ Listening Challenge ❊

Listen and fill in the missing words.

20

1. When we get sick, we [   ] look for a doctor who has lots of experience and who [   ] the latest research and consult her [   ] problem.

2. Companies use Big Data to [   ] advertisements to post on social media, to what age group, at what time of day, [   ].

3. Recently there are [   ] also use machine learning to determine which employees are [   ] and should be fired.

4. Machine-learning applications with [   ] can test car engine performance and even suggest changes that [   ] improve it.

5. Within our lifetimes, [   ] enormous changes in the use of data and machine learning in how we grow crops, as well as [   ] them.

Going Further (for discussion or research)

1. What might be some negative effects of depending on machine learning?

2. How would you feel about using machine learning in your classroom?

CHAPTER *6*

Where the Fish Grow

　画像は養殖中の稚魚に餌を与えている女性。

　魚介類、海藻などの養殖は急増する世界の人口の食料をまかなう貴重な資源となっている。陸地ではすでに牧畜用に相当の土地や水資源が使われていて、海洋に資源を求める動きがさらに増大しているところだ。

　日本では身近な話題だろう。海に行けば種々の養殖の囲いやいかだを目にするだろうし、世界に先駆ける完全養殖マグロ（近大マグロ）や温泉トラフグ養殖の成功、あるいはウナギの稚魚（シラスウナギ）漁獲量などもすぐに報道される……。

Where the Fish Grow

21

Aquaculture—the rearing of fish, shellfish, and seaweed for food—has long been seen as a supplementary means of feeding the burgeoning population of the world. Raising cows, pigs, and even chickens uses valuable land and water, and people have increasingly looked to the ocean as a source of food. Some coastal areas have been turned into "fish farms," with varying degrees of success. But now we need to get 5 serious about other large-scale methods of increasing the world production of fish.

One attempt at this in New Zealand uses traditional know-how. More than a half century ago, the University of Auckland Marine Laboratory presented a controversial idea to a small fishing community facing declining fish catches. The plan was to protect five square kilometers of nearby marine habitat by prohibiting the taking of 10 anything from the sea there: no fish, no lobster, no oysters, no seaweed. Many local people, used to leisure fishing in the area, were vigorously opposed.

●NOTES●

1 **fish, shellfish, seaweed** 食用としての「魚類、貝類、海藻類」。不可算名詞で単数形になる。／ 2 **feeding the burgeoning population**「急増する人口を養う」／ 5 **"fish farms"**「養魚場」／ 6 **production of fish**「魚の生産」／ 10 **fishing community**「魚とりコミュニティ」魚とりと関係する生活をしている人々で構成されている地域。／ 10 **five square kilometers of nearby marine habitat**「近くの海洋生息地 5 平方キロメートル」

✱ Comprehension Check ✱

1. The small fishing community in New Zealand . . .
   a. was eager to support the University of Auckland plan.
   b. wanted to reduce the habitat to two square kilometers.
   c. was accustomed to fishing in the area the university wanted to block off.

22

But the habitat was established, and gradually everyone could see a payoff. By not taking any form of marine life from the reserve, the natural balance of seaweed, lobsters, urchins, and fish returned to normal. Significantly, sea life spread out beyond the boundaries of the protected marine habitat, where local fishers were free to take them. In this case humans were able to assist nature by leaving the natural processes 5 alone; and humans benefited by leaving it that way.

During the last 20 years, the world production of farmed fish has almost quadrupled. Fish farms include water-flooded diked fields and man-made tanks on land, but the vast majority are "near-shore" fisheries. The best-known are the salmon fish farms in the fjords of Norway. With salmon becoming a popular item even in 10 sushi in Japan, the demand for salmon has risen rapidly in recent years, causing unanticipated problems. The two main issues are that there is not enough space and fish-farming pollutes the water. The excrement from millions of the fish foul the water of the fjords. And because the waters of the fjords are shallow and relatively still, those waters become filled with parasites called sea lice. 15

● NOTES ●

1 **payoff**「成果」／2 **form of marine life**「海洋生物の種類」／3 **urchin** [ɚ́ːrtʃin]「ウニ」／7– **has almost quadrupled** [kwɑdrúːpld]「ほぼ4倍になった」／8 **water-flooded diked fields**「水に浸かった堤防地」／8 **man-made tank**「人工のため池」／10 **fjord** [fjɔrd]「フィヨルド」断崖の間に入り込んだ狭い湾。／15 **sea lice**「ウミジラミ」lice は louse の複数形。

✻ *Comprehension Check* ✻

2. The protected habitat . . .

   a. returned to a natural balance of marine life.

   b. expanded its boundaries.

   c. has been eliminated.

3. Today fish farms . . .

   a. consist mostly of fields and tanks filled with water.

   b. are limited in production.

   c. are mostly fisheries not far from shore.

23

    The aquaculture revolution now involves enormous open-ocean experimental fish farms. One American firm is currently employing large open-ocean aquaculture nets off the coast of Hawaii and Panama. But the largest fish farm by far is a frame measuring 68 meters vertically and over 100 meters horizontally built by the Norwegians. It is placed five kilometers off shore in the open ocean, where the water has more oxygen. 5 The stronger currents help wash away the fish excrement. Whereas near-shore farms spread feed on the surface and fish swim up to eat it, the Norwegians' Ocean Farm 1, as it is called, has a unique feeding mechanism. It has valves spaced at various depths below the surface. By feeding the salmon in deeper water, the fish stay there. Sea lice, which prefer shallower waters, don't go down to where the fish are.

As these experimental fish farms scale up their operations, they will learn how to optimize the amount and timing of feeding of the salmon. With enough experience, the operators may well be able to automate huge farms, reducing human involvement. This could well be a major advance in sustaining global fish stocks.

● NOTES ●

1 **open-ocean**「外洋」／2 **is currently employing . . .**「目下…を採用している」／3 **by far**「(最上級、ときには比較級を強めて) はるかに、断然」／7 **Ocean Farm 1** ノルウェイの世界的規模の水産会社 SalMar 社が所有運営している海洋養魚場の第 1 号の名前。／8 **valve**「(給餌用装置の) 弁、バルブ」／12 **optimize**「最適にする」／13 **may wel . . .**「たぶん…だろう」could well . . . もほぼ同じ意味。

✳ *Comprehension Check* ✳

4. Open-ocean fish farms have the advantage of . . .

    a. being beyond any country's control.

    b. making use of stronger currents and water with more oxygen.

    c. keeping fish closer to the surface of the ocean.

5. The advantage of open-ocean over near-shore farms is . . .

    a. the latter create a healthier environment for the fish.

    b. the latter are too expensive to maintain.

    c. the former do not require as much oxygen in the water.

❊ Structure Practice ❊

A. Choose the one underlined word or phrase that should be corrected or rewritten. Then change it so the sentence is correct.

1. The nations of the world need ₁obey the UN Law of the Sea to ₂guarantee that people everywhere have ₃access to clean seas, fish, and other ₄sea life.

   [   ]

2. It comes as ₁no surprise that people who live ₂at coastlines want to protect their areas from both ₃pollution and other people trying to ₄take their fish.

   [   ]

B. Choose the phrase that best completes the sentence.

3. The New Zealand fishing community plan . . .
   a. was supported initially.
   b. prohibited a few forms of sea life.
   c. faced opposition at the beginning.
   d. did not have an impact on leisure fishers.

4. Fish farms in the Norwegian fjords . . .
   a. do not provide fish used in sushi.
   b. have too much space for salmon.
   c. are in deep water.
   d. face issues with excrement in the water.

5. The parasite known as sea lice . . .
   a. do not like to go into deep waters.
   b. cause no harm to salmon fish farms.
   c. can be eliminated by special treatment.
   d. avoid shallow waters.

❊ Listening Challenge ❊

🎧 24 **Listen and fill in the missing words.**

1. By completely [   ] a marine habitat, not only did that habitat recover, but it helped sea life grow [   ] the habitat as well.

2. Local fishers [   ] when it was proposed but [   ] went by they discovered that it worked to their advantage [
      ].

3. The world [   ] farms on valuable land and [
              ] to raise cattle and chickens but we now know that there is a limit to [   ] produce.

4. Countries [   ] have an exclusive economic zone that reaches out 200 nautical miles [   ], including rights to sea life and minerals [   ].

5. New open-ocean [   ] farms set up off the coasts of Hawaii and Panama [   ] feeding fish that are automated and improving the number of fish that [   ].

Going Further (for discussion or research)

1. What political issues exist regarding the Exclusive Economic Zones (EEZ) near Japan?

2. Can fish farms eventually replace open-sea fishing in the future?

Shaping the Future Factory: From Shoes to Aircraft to Body Parts

　3Dプリンターは通常の印刷物と異なり、複製する物体の3次元化されたデータをコンピューター上で作成し、樹脂や金属粉を「インク」として積み重ねて生成する。この方法は「付加製造」と呼ばれる技術としては画期的なものだ。

　画像のような簡単な形状のモノから始まり、現在では多種多様の軽量の商品などが量産可能だ。データさえ共有できれば大規模な設備は必要ないというメリットもある。

　「バイオプリンティング」と呼ばれる分野での利用はまだ初期段階だ。将来的には人間の内臓を生成して治験に応用が可能となり、実験動物の犠牲を減らすことも……

Shaping the Future Factory:
From Shoes to Aircraft to Body Parts

25

The term "3D printing" is part of contemporary vocabulary. Invented in 1983 by American engineer Chuck Hull, 3D-printing machines allow a product to be designed on a computer screen and then "printed," not as a two-dimensional item but as a three-dimensional solid object. This is done by building up successive layers of material, which can be as varied as plastic and steel. The process is also known as additive 5 manufacturing, and it is already turning into reality things that we could only imagine on a computer screen before.

Three-dimensional (3D) printing quickly became a valuable manufacturing tool for creating one-off prototypes. Changes to the parts of a machine, for example, could be made by juggling the 3D printer's software, rather than resetting a combination 10 of tools inside a factory. Initially, this sort of technology was limited to low-volume manufacturing, and elsewhere it could only be applied to crafts like jewelry-making or to the ear buds used with smartphones. In the commercial market, it was good for making lightweight shapes for individual vehicles, but not for high-volume goods. It took too much time to produce them. 15

●NOTES●

1 **3D printing** 3次元のデジタル・モデルを立体物に出現させることを3Dプリンティング（英：3D printing）、三次元造形（さんじげんぞうけい）と呼ぶ。／2 **Chuck Hull** チャック・ハル。1939年生まれ。2014年「国立発明者の殿堂」(National Inventors Hall of Fame)」入り。／4 **solid object**「固形の物体」／4 **building up successive layers of material**「材料の（薄い）層を次々積み重ねる」layers「積層」薄い層の積み重ね。／5 **can be as varied as plastic and steel**「プラスティックやはがねのように、変形されうる」／5– **additive manufacturing**「アディティヴ・マニュファクチャリング、付加製造方法」layersとよばれる薄板を重ね合わせたようなものを製造の元データとして作成し、それに粉体、樹脂、鋼板、紙などの材料を2次元加工することを繰り返す造形法。／11 **tools inside a factory**「工場内の工具」／11– **low-volume manufacturing**「少量生産」high-volume「大量の」／12 **elsewhere**「その他の場では」／12 **crafts like jewelry-making**「宝飾品製作のような仕事」craft 手の技術を要する仕事。／13 **ear bud**「小型イヤホン」／14 **lightweight shape**「軽量の（製品を作るための）型」／14 **individual vehicles**「個人用の乗り物類」次のパラグラフに各種の乗り物についての記述がある。

✳*Comprehension Check*✳

1. Additive manufacturing . . .

    a. produces three-dimensional objects with different materials.

    b. is different from "3D printing."

    c. cannot be designed by computer.

2. Three-dimensional printing . . .
   a. was first valuable in manufacturing prototypes.
   b. depended on adjusting tools in a factory.
   c. did not work well in crafts like jewelry-making.

The reins that have held back additive manufacturing are loosening rapidly. One spurt forward is the development of a new method of creating the soles of sports shoes by the German sportswear company Adidas. Where many German and American manufacturers have until now depended on low-cost factories in Asia to produce the soles of athletic shoes, the new printing technology can be done in automated 5 factories near headquarters. In the past, it took several months to get a design into production. Now it takes a week or less to produce them anywhere in the world.

That also changes the impact of economies of scale. Rather than producing thousands of a product and having to store them in huge warehouses, it is now possible to put the digital design for a part online and have it downloaded to different 10 locations to be printed to order. No extra space is taken by unpurchased parts.

● NOTES ●
1 **The reins that have held back additive manufacturing** 「付加製造法を抑えてきた手綱」／1– **One spurt forward** 「ひとつの急激な前進」／ **headquarters** 既出。「本拠、本部」通例複数扱い。／8 **That also changes the impact of economies of scale.** 「それは量の経済の影響力をも変える」／10 **put the digital design for a part online** 「部品のためのデジタルデザインをオンラインに置く」

✳ *Comprehension Check* ✳

3. Athletic shoe manufacturers are now able to produce soles for shoes . . .
   a. within several months.
   b. in automated factories anywhere.
   c. in low-cost Asian factories.

Polymers were the original materials used in the new printing-type manufacturing, but today metal materials are slowly entering the market. Traditional metal manufacturing has until now depended on taking sheets or blocks of often costly alloys and removing the unnecessary areas, resulting in expensive waste. By adding material rather than subtracting it, the production method saves money because there ⁵ is less waste. The value of savings in manufacturing a car or truck are significant, but they are huge for an aircraft part and gigantic for structural titanium parts for spacecraft.

The medical industry adopted additive manufacturing long ago. Because each person is different, dental implants, metal tooth crowns, and hearing-aid ear buds ¹⁰ were among the earliest individually created products produced. Then there were prosthetic body parts, such as arms and legs.

So-called "bio-printing" is in the early stages of development, but in the near future, it may become possible to bio-print human kidney and liver tissue for screening potential drugs for efficacy. This will reduce the use of test animals. Because the ¹⁵ tissue is human tissue—but not taken from a living human being—results from experiments using it will be more reliable than those from tests on tissue from other species of animals. The potentials of this type of additive manufacturing are literally life-changing.

●NOTES●

1 **Polymer** 「ポリマー」高分子化合物のこと。単量体「モノマー」(monomer) が重合して繰り返し結合をすることによってできる。ポリマーの「ポリ」は「多数」を意味する。プラスチック材料および製品は、高分子化合物「ポリマー」であり、プラスチックの名前には頭に「ポリ」が付く。／3 **has until now depended on taking sheets or blocks of often costly alloys and removing the unnecessary areas** 「今まで多くの場合は高価合金の薄い板や版を要し、不要な部分を取り除くことに依存してきた」／11 **were among the earliest individually created products produced** 「もっとも初期の一つ一つ考案された製品が作り出したものに含まれていた」／14 **for screening potential drugs for efficacy** 「将来性のあるくすりの効き目を検査するために」

✱Comprehension Check✱

4. Before three-dimension printing, manufacturing with metals was . . .

   a. limited.

   b. a way of saving money.

   c. expensive and wasteful.

5. Bio-printing may . . .

   a. create human tissue for testing drug effectiveness.

   b. be used to replace tissue on humans.

   c. not be as good as tissue from other species of animals.

❊ Structure Practice ❊

A. Choose the one underlined word or phrase that should be corrected or rewritten. Then change it so the sentence is correct.

1. It is much ₁less expensive to create a ₂one-off handmade bracelet than to ₃engineer a machine that can produce ₄hundred of bracelets.   [   ]

2. Three-dimensional printing ₁employing human ₂imagination, computer designing, ₃successive layers of different materials, and ₄little else.   [   ]

B. Choose the phrase that best completes the sentence.

3. When it first came into use, three-dimensional printing . . .
   a. worked best with small-quantity manufacturing.
   b. was entirely limited to the making of jewelry.
   c. had little or no connection with computer designs.
   d. was perfect for high-volume production.

4. Because 3D printing could be done in automated factories . . .
   a. low-cost factories were essential for mass production.
   b. it required more time to put designs into full production.
   c. low-volume production did not become essential.
   d. it could be done in any part of the world.

5. A significant difference between the older manufacturing and 3-D printing manufacturing is the switch . . .
   a. to materials that were not available earlier.
   b. from subtracting to adding materials.
   c. from adding metal sheets in the manufacturing process.
   d. to much cheaper metal materials.

❋ Listening Challenge ❋

Listen and fill in the missing words.

1. The [   ] is dependent on a combination of [
   ] designing and materials such as alloys which [   ] in the
   past.

2. [   ] metals like titanium are extremely expensive, money
   is saved by creating [   ] of the material rather than by cutting pieces
   out of [   ] the material.

3. The [   ] bio-printing is that material [   ] could
   be used in experiments [   ] materials from humans.

4. Dental implants and hearing-aid buds [   ] that
   were first created by additive manufacturing because they [
   ].

5. Before long [   ] screen drugs to see if they are effective
   by using bio-printed tissue [   ] human tissue.

Going Further (for discussion or research)

1. Can you think of a way of using 3D printing that has not been mentioned in this
   chapter?

2. If you had such a printer and your choice of materials, what would you like to
   make?

3. Do you believe that making human tissue is ethically acceptable?

CHAPTER 8

Monitor Addiction

　諸君は 1 日に何度スマホ画面をチェックするだろうか。ある調査では 1 日平均で 150 回という報告もある。電車内でも歩行中でもスマホ片手の人間だらけだ。立ち止まった場所が遮断機の内外の勘違いだったとされる衝撃的な死亡事故は他人事ではあるまい。

　ラスベガスのギャンブラーたちの間には「マシンゾーン」という言葉があって、目の前の画面に心身ともに釘付けになり、恍惚の世界に没入する状態になることを言うらしい。

　かくも種々の弊害を伴う、モニター中毒について考えてみよう。専門家の分析や見解はどうなのか、有効な解決策はあるのか……。

Monitor Addiction

Obsession with mobile devices is growing stronger. A 2015 study by Nottingham Trent University showed that 18 to 33-year-olds checked their phone an average of 85 times a day. Another study says that today the average person checks their phone 150 times a day. Regardless of which figure is more accurate, that means a lot of intrusions into your daily life.   5

In this age of hyper-connectivity, many digital addicts are unaware of just how dependent they are on their smartphones—for playing games, checking social networks, and getting information. They check one last time before going to sleep and immediately check again when they wake up. Subway passengers check their phones repeatedly between stations. Office workers use their devices in the toilet.   10 Pedestrians look at something on their phones as they bump into people on busy sidewalks. Obviously that is more important than watching where they are going.

Researchers who study slot-machine gamblers in Las Vegas have found that gamblers talk about "the machine zone." This means a mental state in which their attention is locked into the screen in front of them, and the rest of the world just fades   15 away. It's like a trance or a magnet, they say. It just pulls you in and holds you. You can't get away from it. That is what the casinos aim for. It is also what smartphone apps aim for.

●NOTES●

1– **Nottingham Trent University**「ノッティンガム・トレント大学」イギリスの国立大学。最先端企業との連携に積極的で日本の富士通と連携契約を結んでいる。／6 **hyper-connectivity** インターネット、モバイルテクノロジー、モノのインターネット (IOT) により、人々や組織、モノの相互連携が高まった状態。／8 **one last time**「最後にもう一度」／11 **as they bump into people**「人にぶつかりながら」／12 **that is more important than watching where they are going**「どこを進んでいるかを気をつけるよりそれは大切である」／16 **a trance or a magnet**「夢うつつの状態かひきつけられている状態」

✴ *Comprehension Check* ✴

1. According to the Nottingham Trent University study, younger adults checked their phones . . .

   a. throughout the day.

   b. 85 times a day regardless of where they were.

   c. 85 times a day on average.

2. The "machine zone" that gamblers talk about . . .

    a. is what smartphone apps aim for.

    b. locks your attention on Los Vegas.

    c. is easy to escape from.

30
　　Ask someone who regularly multitasks whether they can really concentrate on several different things at the same time and they usually say yes. They claim that when they are busy, multitasking is the only way to get things done. Research suggests, however, that they are not successfully dealing with the overload of information that multitasking presents. One side effect is a drop-off in ability to concentrate for　5 long periods of time. Another is the tendency to skim, rather than contemplate while reading something serious, like literature or long newspaper articles.

　　What exactly causes users to become addicted to the apps that they access on their mobile monitors? Researchers who study both psychology and computer science refer to the inducing of people to use apps as a form of "behavior design." It is a way　10 of triggering an action that the user is motivated to do, by making it simple. Once the user accomplishes the act, he or she will be tempted to use the app again, and again. The creator of the app "nudges" the user to take action.

● NOTES ●

1 **Ask . . . whether ~**「…に〜かどうか尋ねてごらん」 **multitask** マルチタスクとは複数の仕事を同時に進めること。電算用語では、一台のコンピュータで複数のプログラムを同時に実行すること。／5 **drop-off**「顕著な悪化、減少」／10 **refer the inducing of people to use apps as a form of "behavior design."**「人々にアプリを使用するように誘導することを『行動デザイン』の一つのやりかたと呼んでいる」behavior design「ビヘイビア・デザイン」とは、人々の振る舞いや行動をどのように変えるかという設計。／10 **It is a way of triggering an action that the user is motivated to do**「ユーザーがやる気になる行動をひき起こす方法である」／13 **nudge**「（注意をひくために）肘でそっと突く」

✳ *Comprehension Check* ✳

3. Which statement is NOT true of people who say they can multitask?

    a. They can't concentrate for a long time.

    b. They skim over serious reading material.

    c. They don't believe they are very busy.

4. Creators of smartphone apps make apps simple so that . . .

   a. people will trigger them.

   b. people will nudge them.

   c. people will use them.

🎧
31
    The key is a delivery of dopamine, a pleasurable habit-forming chemical that the brain releases in response to social interactions. If you are vulnerable to social approval, you are drawn in repeatedly to invitations to connect or to get a "like" response. Post a photo, get a positive response from someone, and you get a hit of dopamine. But dopamine is short-lived. Once it dissipates, you want another hit.   5

    One result of this addiction, however, is digital fatigue. With emails to check, Facebook posts to respond to, Instagram photos to upload, and text messages to respond to, the time you might spend unwinding is spent scrolling. And before you are aware of it, you are spending spare hours thinking about how to organize your daily life so you can take great pictures to make others think that your life is happy 10 and exciting. To the contrary, you become stressed and unhappy.

● NOTES ●

1 **delivery of dopamine**「ドーパミンの放出」／1 **pleasurable habit-forming chemical**「気もちの良い習慣性の化学物質」／2 **in response to social interaction**「社会的なふれあいに応じて」／2– **vulnerable to social approval**「社会的な賛同に負けやすい」／3– **are drawn in repeatedly to invitations to connect or to get a "like" response**「人と繋がるための、または『いいね』の応答を得るための誘いに繰り返し引き込まれる」／4 **hit**「（俗語）ハイになること、恍惚；（薬の）1回分」／5 **Once it dissipates**「ひとたび消散してしまうと」／6 **digital fatigue**「デジタル疲れ」／7 **Facebook posts to respond to**「返信するフェイスブックの投稿」／8 **the time you might spend unwinding**「くつろぎに費やせるかもしれない時間」／9 **how to organize your daily life**「毎日の生活を作り上げる方法」

✳ *Comprehension Check* ✳

5. Digital fatigue does NOT come from . . .

   a. trying to make your life seem exciting.

   b. organizing your life so you can upload great photos.

   c. social interactions.

❈ Structure Practice ❈

A. Choose the one underlined word or phrase that should be corrected or rewritten. Then change it so the sentence is correct.

1. A researcher at a busy ₁<u>intersection</u> in Tokyo once ₂<u>recorded</u> the percentage of pedestrians ₃<u>wait</u> for the green light who were checking their smartphone and found that ₄<u>well over</u> half of the people did so.　　　　[　　　　]

2. While ₁<u>certain</u> messages can be checked with a quick skimming ₂<u>over</u> of material and a short response, others ₃<u>required</u> careful reading and concentration in preparing a ₄<u>suitable</u> response.　　　　[　　　　]

B. Choose the phrase that best completes the sentence.

3. When gamblers talk about "the machine zone" they are referring to . . .
   a. a special smartphone app.
   b. selection of a particular slot machine.
   c. being locked out of a game.
   d. a degree of concentration.

4. Behavior design encourages people to . . .
   a. deal with multiple tasks.
   b. connect with others.
   c. concentrate for a long time.
   d. repeat simple actions.

5. The brain releases chemical called dopamine which . . .
   a. does not last a long time.
   b. prevents social interactions.
   c. causes you considerable stress.
   d. ultimately makes you unhappy.

❈ Listening Challenge ❈

Listen and fill in the missing words.

1. Because we have so [   ] and apps that allow us to
   communicate with people we know and [   ], we can
   easily become distracted by trying to [   ] the endless exchange of
   messages.

2. Some people seem [   ] their mobile monitors that they
   carelessly [   ] intersections without checking traffic
   and walk into other pedestrians on sidewalks without [   ].

3. One after another new apps are developed [   ] play games,
   locate places to eat, [   ] trains run, keep us posted regarding the
   latest news, and even [   ] to say into other languages.

4. Given the [   ] contemporary society, it is no wonder
   that both young people and older people [   ] to sort out the
   important from the unimportant and [   ] what they actually need
   to know.

5. People [   ] managing their time seem [   ]
   certain hours to leisure, some to work, and still find time to gain new skills that will
   be [   ].

Going Further (for discussion or research)

1. Do you find connections via messages, posts, and emails to be satisfying? If so,
   why?

2. How have the smartphone and the internet affected contemporary lifestyles?

CHAPTER *9*

Endless Education
—Learning for a Lifetime

　ひと昔前、高等教育は特定の業種のための専門的な職業訓練を受けるか、より高額な生涯賃金が約束される4年間の学部教育を選ぶか、という2つの選択肢があった。この状況は企業のオートメーション化、AI、ロボット工学の進歩により、劇的に変化した。

　自分のキャリアにおいても、生涯学習は必須の要件となる。上記の通り、技術の進歩によって現場に「インテリ」がいる必要はなくなり、職場を奪われてしまいかねない。

　諸処で開講されている「大規模公開オンライン講座」などを利用して、より専門的な分野の学習にチャレンジしていくのも生涯学習が持つ意味の一つでは……。

Endless Education—learning for a lifetime

In previous decades, the main divide in higher education was between those who went through vocational education and came out with specialized training for a vital first job and those who went through four-year college degrees with the promise of higher lifetime earnings. When automation expanded in factories and offices, there was a surge in college graduates, and considerable prosperity. Across the globe, those days are rapidly coming to an end. Today artificial intelligence and robotics are creating the need for an educational revolution that offers new ways to learn and earn. 5

Encouraging people to extend their education into higher-level formal education at the beginning of their lives is not the answer. Specialized training in high school or two-year colleges is not the answer. Taking time out of a career to go back to school is not an answer either. In fact, the whole idea that education concludes with graduation from school has to be thrown out entirely. What is necessary is a shift to lifelong learning. 10

What has happened since roughly 2000 is that the share of high-skilled jobs around the world has been falling, leaving college-educated workers taking on jobs that were once done by less-educated workers. 15

●NOTES●

2 **went through** > go through「（全過程を）終える」／8 **came out** >come out「出てくる」／8 **formal education**「学校教育」／ 10 **Taking time out of a career** take ... out of～「～から…を取る、奪う」

✳ *Comprehension Check* ✳

1. Until now, how many options did high school graduates have before going to work?

   a. Two.   b. Three.   c. Four.

2. The term "lifelong learning" . . .

   a. does not refer to college education.

   b. means schooling after high school.

   c. means going back to school after graduation.

34

That in turn has pushed the less-educated out of the workplace. It is clear that a college degree at the start of a working career is not enough for either group, especially as full-time jobs decrease in number and as job skills need to be updated almost constantly. However, the persistence needed to complete a university degree is a proxy for the fundamental skill of pursuing curiosity to finding an answer to a   5 question, i.e., developing effective learning strategies. That is why many companies require a college degree for jobs that don't seem to require a degree.

What might be a solution? First of all, the world needs to start at the elementary school level, teaching children how to study and how to think. They will need some technical and industry-specific skills, but they will especially need creativity, 10 adaptability, problem-solving skills, and, perhaps most important of all, social skills like empathy and the ability to both cooperate with and lead others. This will help them later in life when they need to gain new skills. Without this, other methods are likely to fail. Through the university level, schools need to promote curiosity, tenacity, and an awareness that students will need to continue learning on their own 15 at least for the rest of their working lives. One way of doing this is through online education.

● NOTES ●
1 **That in turn**「それは次から次へと」／ 3 **decrease in number**「数が減る」／ 5 **proxy for . . .**「…の代わりになるもの」／ 6 **i.e.** [aɪˈiː]「すなわち」ラテン語 id est の略。=that is ／ 15 **tenacity**「粘り強さ」> tenacious ／ 15 **on their own** on one's own「独力で」

✳ *Comprehension Check* ✳

3. To some companies a college degree . . .
   a. shows basic skill in learning strategies.
   b. means having all up-to-date skills and knowledge.
   c. has no more value than graduation from high school.

4. Beginning in elementary school, children need to develop social skills and . . .
   a. technical skills.
   b. prepare for future examinations.
   c. problem-solving skills.

The appeal of massive open online courses (MOOCs) was originally that they offered a wide variety of courses from philosophy to physics to people anywhere in the world. Now MOOCs are leaning toward courses that make students more employable by offering short-term, inexpensive programs to help workers improve their skills. Successful completion of these courses is certified by a "nanodegree" or ⁵ some other proof that the student has learned a specific skill.

There is also room for governments to become involved in lifelong learning. Since January 2016, Singapore has offered every citizen above the age of 25 the equivalent of $345 to pay for any training course provided by several hundred approved providers, including MOOCs, universities, and training schools. Citizens ¹⁰ aged 40 and over are given further subsidies for education. The result is changing the mindset of the population to grasping that learning is a lifelong process.

●NOTES●

1 **MOOCs**「大規模公開オンライン講座」と呼ばれるものでインターネットを通じて無料で世界各国の有名大学などの授業を受けることができる学習環境のこと。／5 **"nanodegree"**「ナノ学位、微小学位」とくに IT 系の分野の特定の技術のみに特化した学位。nano「微小」、単位としての nano（記号 n）は 10⁻⁹。

✱ *Comprehension Check* ✱

5. Which statement is NOT true of MOOCs?
    a. They are available to people around the world.
    b. They help people improve their skills.
    c. They are aimed at university students.

❀ Structure Practice ❀

A. Choose the one underlined word or phrase that should be corrected or rewritten. Then change it so the sentence is correct.

1. Automation and the ₁relocation of factories overseas are two reasons why ₂newcomers to the job markets are finding it hard to ₃obtain employment that pays ₄reasonable well and is fairly stable.   [   ]

2. The ₁importance of having a college ₂degree is not so much that it shows what the person has learned but that it ₃indicate the person has persistence and has learned how to ₄solve problems.   [   ]

B. Choose the word that best completes the sentence.

3. Few people today would . . . that a person's education comes to a halt with graduation from either high school or college.
    a. argue   b. contrast   c. determine   d. follow

4. An employee is likely to fail as a leader if he or she does not . . . some degree of empathy and an ability to encourage cooperation within groups.
    a. complete   b. extend   c. possess   d. proceed

5. It is in the interest of each country's government to . . . lifelong education for its citizens.
    a. subside   b. subsidy   c. subsidies   d. subsidize

❀ Listening Challenge ❀

🎧 **Listen and fill in the missing words.**
36

1. After [   ] and graduating in the top 1 percent of my
    class, when [   ], my grades fell and I was suddenly [
                          ], but I eventually found out what I wanted to learn and [
                          ].

2. It should not [   ] that what one learns in school will not be
    all that you will need [   ] the rest of your life, because as
    times change new skills and [   ].

3. Many people [   ] access to books or dependable
    online reading material [   ] in new fields, picking up the basics
    first and then [   ].

4. [   ] certain types of jobs will disappear or be automated
    completely, one [   ] what kinds of new occupations will
    appear [   ].

5. Several years ago, I [   ] offered by professor at a
    university in Philadelphia, [   ], that I could never
    have attended [   ] in Philadelphia.

Going Further (for discussion or research)

1. What new digital skills do older people need today and how can they gain those
    skills?

2. What types of new jobs do you think will appear in the next decade?

CHAPTER *10*

Drones that Patrol, Deliver, and Teach

　テレビでは頻繁にドローン撮影による映像が流されている。災害現場周辺の調査など、その利用価値は誰もが理解していよう。海中で使えるドローンもあるらしい。

　しかし法整備もままならぬ状態なのに、改良が急ピッチなため、使用目的次第では物議を醸してしまう。オリンピックのセレモニーなどでは平和利用ということで問題はないとしても、この方面の技術革新が「監視」ドローン、ましてや超小型ピンポイント無人攻撃機としての「兵器」ドローンなどに応用されるのはいかがなものか。

　せめて画像の宅配バージョンくらいで打ち止めにして欲しいところかも……。

Drones that Patrol, Deliver, and Teach

Images taken by drones are regularly broadcast on television news. In some cases, drones are used to investigate damage in a disaster in inaccessible areas or assist rescuers in finding people needing help. But those are hardly the only ways that drones are currently in use. Some border on the unnecessary while others have a serious purpose.　　　　　　　　　　　　　　　　　　　　　　　　　5

Among the former are types of submersible drones that are high-tech gadgets for hobby fishermen. One fishing drone goes under water and sends back to a hand-held device a picture of what is going on under the surface. If it spots a fish that the fisherman is interested in, it guides a baited hook to the spot and lets the hook dangle near the fish. One could argue that this is a waste of technology and that it takes the　10 fun out of fishing. Of more commercial value, farmers in the U.S. and other countries are already making use of drones with high-tech cameras to monitor their fields.

●NOTES●

4 **border on . . .**「…に近い、境をなす」／ 7– **hand-held**「片手で持てるサイズの」IT 用語としては持ち運びしやすい小型の端末について用いられる呼称。／ 8 **spot**「見つける」／ 11 **Of more commercial value**「もっと商業的な価値があるものでは」

✳ *Comprehension Check* ✳

1. Drones used for serious purposes do NOT include . . .
    a. access to disaster areas.
    b. spotting fish for hobby fishermen.
    c. assistance to rescue teams.

By guiding a drone across a field, a farmer can detect weeds, locate patches that need more water, and determine where more fertilizer is necessary. Foresters are also using drones to determine where to thin forests to produce larger, healthier trees. Drones provide both the farmer and forester with information they could get in no other way.　　　　　　　　　　　　　　　　　　　　　　　　　5

Already in the news, delivery drones are being developed to distribute ordinary purchases to customers at home. In one early experiment, a drone delivered hot drinks and meals to surfers on a beach in southern California. A potentially more significant type of delivery drone is being tested in Rwanda, a landlocked country with steep hillsides and roads that quickly become impassable in inclement weather. Fixed-wing 10 drones are being developed that can deliver small boxes with parachutes to isolated hospitals. The packages can contain blood for transfusions or life-saving medicine. When roads are cut off due to mudslides or fallen trees, these drones can make the difference between life and death.

●NOTES●
1 **locate patches**「(小区画の) 畑を見つける」／3 **thin forests**「樹木を間引く」／8 **potentially**「可能性を秘めた」／9 **Rwanda** ルワンダ。中央アフリカの国。Republic of Rwand が正式国名。／12 **transfusion**「輸血；注入」> transfuse ／13– **make the difference between life and death**「生と死とを分ける」

✱ *Comprehension Check* ✱

2. Farmers and foresters benefit from drones which provide data for . . .
   a. producing healthier crops and trees.
   b. locating new areas to purchase.
   c. finding new jobs.

3. Drones for delivering medical supplies in Rwanda solve the problems caused by . . .
   a. poverty in the countryside.
   b. roads that are blocked by weather damage.
   c. lack of medical staff.

39   Although experiments are in the beginning stage, drones have potential as a high-tech tool in education. With the recent decrease in both size and cost and a proportionate increase in possible functions, drones are much more than an interesting toy to play with. Even before a drone is put in the air, students in technical classes can learn about circuitry, programming, and construction. They can make alterations 5 and repairs, run test flights, and see what the results are. Students in math classes can make use of drones to calculate speed, measure [=triangulate] positions, and estimate distances and battery life.

    Flying a drone over a particular piece of ground allows students to see how visual perspective is represented on topographical maps. Flying drones above trees, over 10 swamps, and along riverbanks allows students to see plants and animals in their natural habitat.

Should drone operators have the right to fly their devices anywhere? If not, what regulations should governments and aviation agencies establish for drones in populated areas and near airports? Further, how might drones trespass on private 15 property or invade someone's privacy? What would be the proper way for industry, government and individual citizens to regulate the use of drones? Drones and the remote controls that guide them are fascinating in many ways—and we need to take them seriously.

● NOTES ●

3 **proportionate increase in possible functions**「見込みのある機能のつりあった増加」／ 5 **circuitry**「回路」／ 5 **alteration**「改変、変更」／ 7 **triangulate**「三角測量で測量する」／ 10 **topographical map**「地形図」／ 15 **how might drones trespass on private property or invade someone's privacy**「なんとドローンは、私有地に侵入したり、誰かのプライバシーを侵したりする可能性があることだろうか」

✳ *Comprehension Check* ✳

4. Which statement is NOT true regarding drones in school education?

   a. Drones are too expensive for schools to buy.

   b. Drones can be used in technical classes.

   c. Drones can be a teaching tool in math classes.

5. According to the article, the best way for governments, industries, and individuals to regulate drone use . . .

   a. is to leave it up to the government to decide.

   b. is to leave it up to drone operators to work out.

   c. remains to be seen.

❈ Structure Practice ❈

A. Choose the one underlined word or phrase that should be corrected or rewritten. Then change it so the sentence is correct.

1. Natural disasters often cause ₁<u>immediate</u> damage to infrastructure that cannot be ₂<u>detect</u> on the ground, making drones a ₃<u>highly</u> valuable tool for finding where trouble is and who is ₄<u>affected</u>.   [   ]

2. Delivery of ₁<u>medical</u> to hospitals in ₂<u>faraway</u> ₃<u>locations</u> is just one of several highly significant services that drones are capable of ₄<u>providing</u>.
                                                                            [   ]

B. Choose the word or phrase that best completes the sentence.

3. To prevent . . . of privacy there should be regulations regarding the use of zones in areas where people live.
    a. deliveries   b. invasions   c. transfusions   d. tresspasses

4. Drones can be used to . . . linear distances through areas with thick forests.
    a. calculate   b. dangle   c. evaluate   d. regulate

5. After the electricity was . . . we had to depend on candles to see things at night.
    a. found out   b. sent back   c. cut off   d. taken away

❈ Listening Challenge ❈

🎧 **Listen and fill in the missing words.**
40

1. The beach [   ] from places to eat that surfers enjoy the
    novelty of having lunches [   ] by drones.

2. Continuous heavy rain [   ] of trees on the hillside and
    the ground [   ] gave way and slid down [
              ] valley.

3. Some [   ] as hobbies [   ] more fun if
    drones are used, but [   ] a drone might take away the pleasure of doing
    it without help.

4. Satellites cameras [   ] of large areas of land, but
    the drones [   ] on the details since they are taken [
                    ].

5. During my [   ] when I was seven years old, I was
    [   ] from the window, and [   ].

Going Further (for discussion or research)

1. How should we regulate the use of drones?

2. Should drones be allowed over areas where people live?

CHAPTER 11

Energy Transition

　画像はアメリカ、テキサス州のスピンドルトップ油田（1901 年）

　20 世紀は石油に翻弄された時代でもある。石油戦争（中東戦争。古くは日米の太平洋戦争もこの類に含まれるだろう）、石油流出（今も後を絶たない）、石油ショック（中東戦争が起因）。しかし今世紀に至っても未だに石油がエネルギー源としては第 1 位だ。

　地球上で異常気象が頻発し、原因は温室効果ガスの増加によるものだというコンセンサスは得られてきた。電力をまかなうために、化石燃料に代わってソーラーシステムや風力、波力、地熱発電などが利用されてはいるが、それぞれに制約が付いてまわる……。

Energy Transition

The twentieth century was heavily influenced by oil in several ways: oil wars, oil spills, and oil shocks. Unfortunately, despite rapid change in everything else in the twenty-first century, energy markets are changing at a snail's pace. In 2014, oil still accounted for 31% of the global energy supply, compared with 29% for coal, and 21% for natural gas. Rivals to these fossil fuels together contributed little more than 5 1%.

In that year, it was predicted that the first fossil fuel to suffer would be coal, then oil, and, last of all, natural gas. Natural gas was believed to be the best candidate for survival because it is relatively clean. With natural gas and renewable energy sources, many predicted, the global energy system might make a fundamental change. 10

Nonetheless, the "energy transition" is picking up speed across the globe, regardless of how much coal, gas, and oil individual countries have. This transition to wind and solar energy, electricity grids, batteries, and more experimental clean-energy sources has already set off a global competition.

● NOTES ●

1– **oil spills**「(事故などによる海への)石油流出」/ 2 **oil shocks**「オイルショック、石油ショック」石油価格の大幅な引き上げによる世界経済の大混乱、石油危機ともいう。1974 年に第 1 次オイルショック、1979 年に第 2 次オイルショックがあった。/ 5 **fossil fuels**「(石油・石炭・天然ガスなど)化石燃料」/ 5 **little more than**「~にすぎない」/ 13 **electricity grids**「電力網」/ 14 **set off**「引き起こす」

✳ *Comprehension Check* ✳

1. Which statement is true?
    a. Clean-energy fuels are the main suppliers of energy.
    b. In 2014 natural gas supplied more global energy than oil.
    c. Oil remained the largest supplier of energy in 2014.

2. The fossil fuel that may survive is . . .
    a. natural gas.
    b. oil.
    c. coal.

42

The energy transition is a geopolitical contest to see who can produce its own energy and who can develop the best technology. Renewable energy still produces only 8% of the world's electricity, and much less of the energy needed to heat, cool, and transport. The appeal of solar power is that it is becoming cheaper, but only as a niche energy source. Solar panels cannot be turned on and off. They flood the 5 electricity market when the sun is shining brightly and that makes prices drop, but only in the daytime. Batteries could help remedy the situation. For the moment, however, no one has invented a lithium-ion battery that is capable of storing solar energy for long periods.

Part of the needed transition will be the creation of interconnected power systems. 10 Those who have extra clean energy would be able to share it with those who lack it. Doing this would require more cross-border coordination and more high-voltage power lines. Such cooperation is vulnerable to political issues between nations, especially if power lines cross several nations.

● NOTES ●

1 **geopolitical**「地政学の」地理的条件が政治や外交政策に与える影響を研究するもの。／2 **renewable energy**「再生可能エネルギー」／5 **niche**「すき間の」／12– **high-voltage power lines**「高圧送電線」

✳ *Comprehension Check* ✳

3. Solar power . . .

    a. is becoming less expensive but is hard to store.

    b. can be switched on and off.

    c. is easily store for use at night.

43

Another obstacle is the search for and excavation of cobalt and rare earths which are used in lithium-ion batteries and in renewable-energy devices such as wind turbines. Where geopolitical power struggles used to be based on oil, the new struggle will be over cobalt and rare earths.

The transition to clean energy is, of course, driven by the need for serious efforts 5 to tackle global warming. That means every nation will need to expand the use of clean energy sources from electricity to uses in heating, transportation and industrial processes. Regions with unfavorable climates may need to construct high-voltage transmission lines to bring in clean energy from long distances away. Collaboration

will also be needed in sharing technology. Breakthroughs in solar energy storage will 10
require a breakthrough that no single nation is likely to bring about.

　To depoliticize energy, both super-grids and mini-grids will be necessary. Super-grids allow distant nations and regions to share energy—if they are politically friendly. Mini-grids involving wind and solar power, small-scale hydropower and thermal power, and wind power allow small-scale producers to keep local supplies stable, 15 regardless of political events far away. It is difficult to predict how the transition will take place, but few deny that the change will be fast.

● NOTES ●

1 **rare earths**「レアアース（希土類元素）」レアメタルのうち 17 元素の総称。／ 3 **where**「～であるのに」／ 7 **uses**「用途」／ 12 **depoliticize**「～から政治色を取り去る」

✽ Comprehension Check ✽

4. Lithium-ion batteries require . . .

　　a. power from wind turbines.

　　b. rare earths and minerals.

　　c. a decrease in global warming.

5. The global energy transition will . . .

　　a. require shared technology and cooperation between nations.

　　b. make nations work together and cooperate.

　　c. allow each nation to be independent in energy.

❊ Structure Practice ❊

A. Choose the one underlined word or phrase that should be corrected or rewritten. Then change it so the sentence is correct.

1. Oil ₁<u>spills</u> from ships, trucks, and pipelines are regular topics in the media, but the ₂<u>explode</u> of the Deepwater Horizon well in the Gulf of Mexico and all of the oil that ₃<u>leaked from</u> that was of a different ₄<u>magnitude</u>.   [   ]

2. We know that automobile gasoline prices are ₁<u>vulnerable</u> during disasters, so we can ₂<u>assume</u> that the same would be true ₃<u>to</u> electricity that is ₄<u>generated</u> by wind, wave, and sunlight.   [   ]

B. Choose the word that best completes the sentence.

3. New sources of fossil fuels like oil, natural gas, and coal have . . . attention from companies that profit from these resources.
   a. attached   b. drawn   c. rejected   d. yielded

4. The creation of an inexpensive lithium-ion battery, or an equivalent, would make solar energy a more . . . source of energy for local power grids.
   a. comparable   b. dependable   c. inventive   d. renewable

5. Transmission of power to places where the climate does not allow clean energy sources involves not only technology but may also involve. . . agreements between different nations.
   a. appeal   b. decreased   c. political   d. thermal

❊ Listening Challenge ❊

🎧 **Listen and fill in the missing words.**
44
   1. Following [   ], we came to realize [   ] to have batteries for lamps and radios, gas canister stoves, as well as stocks of [   ] meals.

2. In the countryside [   ] high-voltage power lines [
          ], rise up mountain slopes, and [   ].

3. Most people [   ] clean energy but [   ]
   are willing to pay [   ] they pay for fossil fuels.

4. Power grids [   ] mini-grids that transmit [
          ] turbines and solar panels and super-grids that transmit huge amounts of
   power even [   ] different nations.

5. One [   ] sources of power was waterfalls, [
          ] with water wheels, used for grinding wheat, [
   ], and even sawing marble into blocks.

Going Further (for discussion or research)

1. How long do you think it will be before fossil fuels provide less than half of our
   sources of energy?

2. What are the negatives and positives of electric vehicles?

3. Ethiopia and Egypt disagree about who controls the waters of the Nile River, which
   is a source of energy. What are the issues involved?

CHAPTER 12

Artificial Intelligence —Decision Making by Humans and the Competition

　AI ブームの先鞭をつけたのはアマゾンだ。2006 年にネット上で安価なオンラインサービスを開始し、翌年アップルが初代アイフォンを発売。その後同種のサービスはさらに安価になって普及し、企業はビッグデータと呼ばれる膨大な情報を蓄積していった。

　そのデータベースを、AI が「予測する人工知能」として、人間には発想不可能な、一見無関係な項目同士の相関関係を示すなどの威力を発揮するようになった。

　機械学習「ディープラーニング」によってさらに進化した AI が、診断からオペまで主導して外科医に指示を与える。そんなドラマの話も現実になるかもしれない……。

Artificial Intelligence
—Decision Making by Humans and the Competition

The artificial intelligence (AI) boom began when Amazon in 2006 began selling cheap computing over the internet and when Apple in 2007 released the first iPhone. Since that time computing has become cheaper than ever, almost every company has some operations online, and sensors are bringing in enormous amounts of data from more sources. Businesses from agriculture to aviation, are looking to AI as a   5 marketing and production tool. They use it to look at current customer choices to figure out where to put their resources in advertising, and what products to make.

As part of deep learning and machine intelligence, artificial intelligence is basically a series of advanced statistics-based exercises. Computer programs review the past in order to indicate the most likely future. For individuals, the most familiar   10 application of AI is in personal-assistant software. The first examples of these were like digital secretaries. The next generation has gone a step further into what is called "predictive intelligence."

●NOTES●

1 **Amazon in 2006 began selling cheap computing over the internet** アマゾンが 2006 年に企業向けに公開したクラウド・コンピューティング・サービスのこと。／4 **sensors** ここでいうセンサーとはデータの蓄積や変換などを処理する機能をもったもの。／7 **figure out**「計算する」／7 **put their resources in advertising**「資金を宣伝にかける」／8 **deep learning**「深層学習；ディープ・ラーニング」人間が手を加えなくてもコンピュータが自動的に大量のデータからそのデータの特徴を発見する技術のこと。／8 **machine intelligence**「機械知能；人工知能」／9 **a series of advanced statistics-based exercises**「高度な統計学に基づいた演習の連続」」／11 **personal-assistant**「個人秘書」／13 **predictive intelligence**「予測知能」

✸ Comprehension Check ✸

1. The cost of computing has become . . .

  a. enormous as more companies use online operations.

  b. less expensive in the twentieth century.

  c. a heavy burden on customers.

2. Which of the following is NOT true of artificial intelligence?

  a. It is unable to predict what products might be successful.

  b. It is not used to analyze past customer activity.

  c. It is not used as a marketing tool in various businesses.

Drawing on personal information, email, location data, and internet links, these new assistants are beginning to anticipate what an information user needs. The app in the phone initiates the process by notifying the human user, rather than waiting for the human user to ask for help. Its goal is to provide the right information at the right time. It might warn us about a change in the weather, the stock market, or public ⁵ transportation stoppages, each a helpful bit of information.

The predictive power of AI has been put to the test in the game of Go, and the computer program has usually defeated its human opponents. It does so by employing the type of AI called machine learning, in which computers teach complicated tasks to themselves. The program first analyzes thousands of past games between human ¹⁰ opponents, learning the rules and strategies. It then refines the strategies by playing against itself. In other words, it learns to play quickly without any human assistance. To the contrary, it can teach humans new strategies that no human genius in history has thought of before.

● NOTES ●
   7 **the game of Go**「囲碁」

✱ *Comprehension Check* ✱

3. New personal-assistant software . . .
   a. provides information that might be helpful to the user.
   b. waits for the user to request help.
   c. focuses on giving information about the past.

Researchers are looking to AI to assist in analyzing enormous amounts of data in order to assess options without human oversight. Dr. Shinya Yamanaka, known for research on iPS (induced pluripotent stem) cells, sees AI as a means of analyzing data on the human genome and checking the safety of iPS cells in regenerative medicine. There is a limit to what human knowledge and experience can do, and he believes AI ⁵ can more effectively search for up-to-date research results and databases to confirm that there are no potential negatives in the transplantation of iPS cells.

Deep learning is known for the superhuman capacity it has in certain forms of image recognition. One type of image is taken from radiological systems in hospitals

which are used to determine whether a tumor is malignant or benign, which could 10
reduce unnecessary surgery as well as save lives.

One potential downside to this fast-developing AI is that although it may reduce cost, it could threaten workers' jobs, benefiting only a select few. So-called "job polarization" might eliminate middle-skill jobs in manufacturing and leave only low-skill, low-paying, jobs and highly paid, high-skill jobs such as senior managers, 15 architects, chemical engineers, and book editors.

● NOTES ●

2 **assess options without human oversight** 「人間にありがちな見落としなしに選択肢を判断する」／3 **pluripotent** 「多分化能の；多能性の」pluri-「多数の」／4 **genome** [dʒíːnoum]「ゲノム」／8– **it has in certain forms of image recognition** 「特定の形状の画像認識における」／9 **radiological systems** 「放射線システム」radiology「放射線」／10 **whether a tumor is malignant or benign** 「腫瘍が悪性か良性か」

✱ *Comprehension Check* ✱

4. Dr. Shinya Yamanaka believes AI . . .

   a. can help researchers by analyzing data rapidly.

   b. is slower than humans in analyzing research results.

   c. can create IPS cells.

5. One benefit of AI is . . .

   a. it can recognize whether tumors are malignant or not.

   b. it can reduce the number of jobs humans can do.

   c. it may reduce the jobs performed by architects.

Structure Practice

A. Choose the one underlined word or phrase that should be corrected or rewritten. Then change it so the sentence is correct.

1. The more $_{1}$frequent we use $_{2}$certain computer programs, the better those programs get in $_{3}$anticipating what we might want or $_{4}$be interested in. [ ]

2. Computer programs $_{1}$gather information from $_{2}$masses of human users, $_{3}$analyzes that data and, without being asked, place suggestions $_{4}$in front of individual users. [ ]

B. Choose the word that best completes the sentence.

3. Small laptops today possess the same computing . . . of the much larger computers that were common two decades ago.
   a. anticipation　　b. capacity　　c. recognition　　d. stoppage

4. As we continue using computer programs, machine learning gathers data on our behavior and develops ways to . . . the process that we need to accomplish given tasks.
   a. eliminate　　b. initiate　　c. refine　　d. transfer

5. Despite the likelihood that artificial intelligence may reduce the number of jobs that humans can perform, the . . . is that medical analysis like image recognition could save lives.
   a. upper　　b. upside　　c. up-to-date　　d. upward

Listening Challenge

48 **Listen and fill in the missing words.**

1. As human beings, we have [ ] to absorb information and make [ ] about the future with [ ].

2. [   ] that artificial intelligence is impressive, [
          ] because it often shows [   ] in under-
   standing what we see and hear.

3. As [   ] AI's predictive power in Go, machine learning
   [   ] learns from humans but also [   ].

4. One [   ] artificial intelligence is that it is [
          ] options that in all likelihood human beings [   ].

5. We ought [   ] while AI may lead to advances in society,
   it is morally neutral and [   ] lead to destructive ideas.

Going Further (for discussion or research)

1. What additional uses of artificial intelligence were not mentioned in the passage?

2. What would human life be like in a world built entirely around artificial intelligence?

CHAPTER *13*

Oceans of Plastic

　プラスチックは安価で軽量で加工も容易なので、おそらく世界で最も利用されている素材だ。毎年３億２千万トンという恐るべき生産量を誇る。プラゴミは自国内でのリサイクルに取り組む姿勢も見えつつあるが、「非生分解性」のプラスチック投棄問題は深刻だ。

　海洋生物がプラスチックを誤飲して死に至っている映像などは見るに耐えまい。またマイクロプラスチックと呼ばれる、海流に乗って漂流するプラゴミが劣化・崩壊してできる微細なプラスチック粉体は、プランクトン、魚類を経て、食物連鎖としてすでに人体にも入ってきているという。因果応報というところだろうか……。

Oceans of Plastic

49

Plastics are inexpensive, lightweight, and adaptable, and they are arguably the dominant materials of the global economy. Every year some 320 million tons of plastic are produced, and within the next twenty years, production of plastics is anticipated to double, and there is a problem. Currently only 14% of all plastic packaging is actually collected and recycled after it is used. Some is incinerated. The remainder is 5
left somewhere in the environment, either in landfill or in the natural environment.

Some governments and manufacturers are changing the way they produce, process and recycle plastics. There are growing efforts to first of all produce only plastics that will be fully reusable in some way, completely recyclable, or compostable in a process that is commercially feasible. That becomes economically impracticable, 10
however, for the third of current plastic items that either are very small or come in multi-material units made of several different materials.

Government policy makers can help regulate the use of some plastic items by either banning or requiring consumers to pay for plastic shopping bags. They will, in the future, have to force industry to replace packaging that includes chemicals that 15
pose a risk to humans and other living things.

● NOTES ●

5 **the remainder**「残りのもの」／9 **compostable**「堆肥化の可能な」compost「堆肥」／10 **impracticable**「(実際的な見地から) 非常に難しい」

✳ *Comprehension Check* ✳

1. Which of the following statements is true?
   a. Plastic production will decrease by 14 percent in twenty years.
   b. There will be less plastic production in the next twenty years.
   c. More used plastic will be left in the environment.

2. Plastics that cannot be reused or recycled include . . .
   a. multiple-material items.
   b. compostable material.
   c. expensive material.

Mandatory collection and sorting of drink bottles and steel and aluminum cans is fairly successful in some countries in Europe, but governments will have to enforce laws that make producers responsible for the entire product life cycle of plastics.

When plastics end up somewhere in the environment, one portion ends up in the oceans. Three fifths of the plastic produced is less dense than seawater, so it can be 5 transported by surface currents and wind, ending up on coastlines or floating in the water. Some of this ends up in ocean gyres.

The Great Pacific Ocean Garbage Patch, between Hawaii and California, is the appalling poster child of the worldwide problem of plastic in the waters of the world. This floating junkyard is estimated to cover an area of 1.6 million square kilometers. 10 It is composed of some 79,000 tons of plastic, which does not biodegrade.

●NOTES●

3 **entire product life cycle of plastics**「プラスティックの製品ライフスタイル全体」／4 **end up somewhere in the environment**「最後には自然環境のどこかに行くことになる」／5 **less dense than seawater**「海水より比重が軽い」／7 **ocean gyres**「海洋渦」gyre [dʒaɪ.ɚ]「還流」／8 **The Great Pacific Ocean Garbage Patch**「太平洋ゴミベルト」／9 **poster child**「ポスターチャイルド」広告のポスターに使用するイメージキャラクターのこと。／11 **biodegrade**「（微生物によって）生分解する」biodegradable「生分解性の」

✳ *Comprehension Check* ✳

3. The Great Pacific Garbage Patch . . .
    a. is composed of non-biodegradable plastic.
    b. is located along the coastline.
    c. contains 1.6 million tons of plastic.

Some of it originated in the Great Tohoku Earthquake and Tsunami disaster. But the vast majority consists of consumer products such as bags and plastic bottles from land, nets from fishing vessels, and commercial containers. This great whorl is constantly growing. It is not within any country's EEZ, so it is not the sole responsibility of any country. But the entire world suffers from it, and will continue 5 to do so.

This whorl is the focal point of an even larger danger. Scientists estimate that by the year 2050, there could be more plastic in the ocean than there is fish by weight. Plastic in the oceans is not biodegradable. Taking plastic items out of the ocean is one necessary tactic in solving the issue, but there is a second, equally worrying, problem. 10

Small pieces of plastic end up in the stomachs of fish. Just as the world is growing ever more dependent on the oceans for food, sea life is being endangered by plastic as it enters the food chain. Fish and sea birds ingest bits of plastic and it eventually kills them. Large fish and mammals ingest both these fish and the plastic floating in the water. What goes around comes around.

15

●NOTES●

4 **EEZ** 「排他的経済水域」天然資源の調査・開発や漁業活動の管理などの権利を沿岸国に認める水域。沿岸から 200 カイリ（約 370 キロメートル）までの範囲を EEZ として設定できる。*Exclusive Economic Zone* ／ 11 **Just as . . .** 「まさに…だが」

✱ *Comprehension Check* ✱

4. Which statement is NOT true regarding the Great Pacific Garbage Patch?

    a. It is mostly material from the Great Tohoku disaster.

    b. The responsibility for cleaning it up belongs to no single country.

    c. This floating junkyard is not sinking.

5. Plastics in the ocean . . .

    a. biodegrade slowly.

    b. can end up in the food chain.

    c. don't affect many people.

❈ Structure Practice ❈

A. Choose the one underlined word or phrase that should be corrected or rewritten. Then change it so the sentence is correct.

1. Now that stores in Japan ₁charges a small fee for plastic bags to carry ₂purchases in, more ₃customers seem to ₄be carrying eco-bags when they go shopping.

   [   ]

2. When you ₁separate your trash ₂according to your city's guidelines, you may ₃astonished at what a large percentage of your ₄weekly garbage is plastic.

   [   ]

B. Choose the word that best completes the sentence.

3. . . . some encouragement, the average consumer would continue to carry each purchase in a convenient, free plastic bag.
   a. Although   b. Excepting   c. Unless   d. Without

4. It is . . . that by mid-century there will be as much plastic in the oceans as there is fish, if we were to weigh them.
   a. dominated   b. estimated   c. ingested   d. regulated

5. The Great Pacific Ocean Garbage Patch . . . some material from the Great Eastern Japan Disaster.
   a. composes   b. consists   c. includes   d. involves

❈ Listening Challenge ❈

🎧 **Listen and fill in the missing words.**
52

1. It has always [   ] that people believe it is [

   ] drinks in plastic bottles when water is available [

   ].

2. The Japanese furoshiki, [   ], is the perfect way to carry many things because it is [   ], and attractive as well.

3. Just as humans [   ] of how they pollute the land and air, they are now realizing that they have to [   ], too.

4. [   ] compostable or recyclable or [   ], we ought to consider [   ] eliminated from the planet.

5. It [   ] or ethically acceptable for advanced nations to [   ] to developing countries and [   ].

Going Further (for discussion or research)

1. How do you think the world should deal with the Great Pacific Ocean Garbage Patch?

2. Have you recently changed a habit that might help the environment?

CHAPTER *14*

Active Participation

　運動は健康を維持するのに欠かせない。WHO によれば、世界の成人の４人に１人は運動不足だということだ。また一般的に、運動不足は感染症を除く病気に対しては、抵抗力を弱めてしまうとされている。要は運動するしないの問題ではなく、病気を避けたいかどうかの問題なのだ。

　運動が必要だといっても、必ずしもフィットネスクラブなどで規準に沿ったプログラムをこなそうということではない。買い物がてらに遠回りで散歩したり、オフィスで立ったまま仕事したりなど（ヘミングウエイばりに）、いろいろ工夫はできるだろう……。

Active Participation

53
　　Ernest Hemingway may not seem to be a paragon of health-consciousness, because of his reputation for spending a lot of time in bars. But according to recent research in the medical journal *The Lancet*, his posture when he wrote during the daytime was spot-on: he stood at his desk.

　　The Lancet is one of the world's top-class medical journals, so we ought to take ⁵ their research seriously when they talk about the importance of an active lifestyle in the prevention of diseases. The World Health Organization (WHO) lends support to this view with its contention that, around the world, at least one in four adults is not active enough. These and other sources say clearly that physical activity is an equal partner in preventive strategies for non-communicable diseases. It is not just a matter ¹⁰ of whether or not one should participate in physical activity or not. It is a matter of whether or not you want to avoid disease.

●NOTES●

3 *The Lancet*『ランセット』世界的に権威のあるイギリスの医学雑誌。／4 **spot-on**「ぴったりの」／4 **he stood at his desk** ヘミングウェイは机に向かって立ったままで仕事をすることが多かった。／7 **lend support to . . .**「…に指示を加える」／9 **sources**「資料；情報源」通例複数形。／10 **non-communicable diseases**「非感染性の病気」

✱ *Comprehension Check* ✱

1. In the first paragraph, health-consciousness is connected with . . .
   a. Ernest Hemingway.
   b. writing.
   c. standing at a desk.

2. According to *The Lancet*, an active lifestyle is connected with . . .
   a. medical research.
   b. disease prevention.
   c. communicable diseases.

54
　　It is important to grasp that "physical activity" is not identical with "exercise." Exercise is a subcategory of physical activity. It is structured, repetitive, and planned,

and its purpose is to at least maintain—if not improve—some component of physical fitness. For students and office workers, this type of activity is often hard to schedule. "Physical activity," on the other hand, is bodily movement that is carried out by 5 skeletal muscles that require spending energy, which can be done while working, doing chores, traveling, or participating in recreation. In other words, it does not have to be a separate event. It can be incorporated into regular activities during the day.

WHO suggests that people 18 to 64 years should do at least 75 minutes of vigorous physical activity throughout the week. That's all fine and good, you may say, "But 10 when I'm busy. It's not possible to do much physical activity, much less exercise." Perhaps it will stimulate you to take action if you know that research shows that sitting all day, at home or in the office, is approximately as dangerous as smoking or being overweight.

● NOTES ●
1 **identical with . . .**「…に等しい。同じ」／2 **subcategory**「下位区分」／2 **structured**「体系化された」／3 **some component of physical fitness**「肉体的な良好状態のある要素」／7 **it does not have to be a separate event**「単独のイベントである必要はない」／11 **much less**「いわんや：ましてなおさら」

✱ *Comprehension Check* ✱

3. "Physical activity" is . . .
   a. not just structured, planned exercise.
   b. not done while participating in work or chores.
   c. not part of everyday activities.

4. According to WHO . . .
   a. vigorous activity should be done three times a week.
   b. sitting all day is unhealthy.
   c. being busy is good for health.

🎧
55
For those of us feel that we can't set aside a "special time" to do physical exercise, there are several alternatives worth considering. Even walking exercises various muscles, improves metabolism, and helps circulation. Further, walking can more easily be built into a busy daily schedule. Take the long way when you go shopping. Keep in mind that it takes 60 to 75 minutes of moderate-intensity exercise to undo the 5

damage of sitting for at least eight hours a day.

Then there is the option of reducing your total sitting time. You may not have time to walk but you can use a desk that allows you to work either standing or sitting. The desks can be adjusted for height, so that the user can stand part of the time, then lower the top and sit part of the time. Workers who stand even part of the day report 10 that they feel better, it improves communication with others, and it stimulates new idea and fresh perspectives. Hemingway must have been onto something.

●NOTES●
2 **walking exercises various muscles**「ウォーキングは様ざまな筋肉を働かせる」／3 **metabolism**「(新陳)代謝」／6 **undo the damage of ...**「…のダメージを取り戻す」／12 **onto ...**「…に気づいて、分かって」

✱ *Comprehension Check* ✱

5. Walking and standing part of the day is . . .
    a. better than vigorous physical activity.
    b. impossible for people like Hemingway.
    c. good for health and mental stimulation.

❀ Structure Practice ❀

A. Choose the one underlined word or phrase that should be corrected or rewritten. Then change it so the sentence is correct.

1. Ernest Hemingway ₁<u>not known</u> ₂<u>for maintaining</u> a ₃<u>healthy lifestyle</u> although he is famous as ₄<u>a world-class</u> writer.   [   ]

2. ₁<u>Skeletal muscles</u> that use some amount of energy ₂<u>contributes to</u> the physical activity that ₃<u>differs from</u> what we ₄<u>refer to as</u> exercise.   [   ]

B. Choose the word that best completes the sentence.

3. I try to take even a short walk each day in order to . . . physical activity into my daily routine.
    a. adjust   b. contend   c. incorporate   d. maintain

4. Walking between two subway stops takes . . . twenty minutes.
    a. approximate   b. approximated
    c. approximately   d. approximates

5. . . . the importance of physical activity in maintaining good health, it is surprising that all of us don't do more of it.
    a. Assume   b. Conclude   c. Given   d. Suspecting

❀ Listening Challenge ❀

🎧 **Listen and fill in the missing words.**
56
1. Attempting to cram [   ] exercise into one afternoon's activity [   ] the wisest thing to attempt, so divide it up [   ].

2. You might want [   ] that wearing a mask [   ] and all of the people around you [   ].

3. His sister [   ] he join her yoga class once a week, but because most of the members are women he doesn't [   ] to follow up [   ].

4. [   ] of time, she learned enough about rugby to enjoy watching it and [   ] when her country's side [   ] the goal.

5. On some occasions, when you [   ], the best thing you can do is go for a walk and [   ] for a short while.

Going Further (for discussion or research)

1. Do you get as much physical activity as you need to stay healthy?

2. Is remote learning or remote work good for your mental and physical health? Why?

CHAPTER 15

Life during a Pandemic

　パンデミックの始まりは 14 世紀に大流行したペスト（黒死病）だとされている。今世紀の新型コロナ (Covid-19) も永久に人類史に刻まれることになるだろう。

　今回のパンデミックでの各国の対応や国民の反応はさまざまで、国民性や時の国家の指導者、それに世代による相違などは注目に値しよう。

　キャンパスには入れないわ、オンライン授業に翻弄されるわ、バイトはなくなるわで途方に暮れた学生もハンパなかろう。未曾有の事態に「船頭多くして船山に上る」状態は致し方ない面もあろうが、パンデミックでいや増した格差パンデミックは何とかならんか。

Life during a Pandemic

Outbreaks of serious diseases have struck the world since ancient times, the worst of them being the bubonic plague, known as the Black Death. Spreading from central Asia through Constantinople, it reached most parts of Europe between 1347 and 1349, causing widespread panic. Attempts to fight the spread were useless. In Europe alone, it killed more than one quarter of the population. 5

Fast forwarding to 1918, another pandemic struck the world. This influenza virus devastated the populations of the world causing at least fifty million deaths worldwide, and possibly twice that figure. A century later, we are dealing with the Covid-19 pandemic, and we will continue to deal with it for the foreseeable future.

Because fear of contagion has prompted restrictions and even lockdowns in some 10 parts of the world, much of public life has come to a halt. The result has been a decline of excitement, increased loneliness, lower energy levels, lethargy, sadness, and depression. Replacing our desire for company is a fear of crowds and avoidance of anyone coughing or not wearing a mask.

●NOTES●

2 **bubonic plague**「(中世ヨーロッパで多くの命を奪った) 鼠蹊 (そけい) 腺ペスト」／7 **devastated**「壊滅させた」／8 **possibly twice that figure** = that figure is possibly twice「2 倍の数値になっているかもしれない」／10 **contagion**「感染」

❋ *Comprehension Check* ❋

1. Which statement is true?
    a. The Black Death spread until 1918.
    b. Covid-19 is a variety of the bubonic plague.
    c. It was impossible to stop the Black Death.

2. According to the reading, the Covid-19 pandemic . . .
    a. will continue for some time.
    b. has killed more people than the 1918 influenza epidemic.
    c. is more dangerous than the bubonic epidemic.

It is easy to focus on the negatives, but there are some potential positives as well. One is that we have come to appreciate doctors, nurses, and medical researchers much more than before. We have certainly become more aware of their altruism, the importance of public health, and the need for government support of all who are involved. 5

Another positive is that because time with other people has diminished, we appreciate having such occasions more. Where previous pandemics—including the scarlet fever pandemic—boosted the importance of telephones, the current one has promoted the value of Zoom, FaceTime, and other forms of remote communication. While seeing someone on a monitor is not as enjoyable as seeing them in person, we 10 can meet people in distant locations and communicate with them more easily.

Small businesses, including restaurants and drinking places, have lost customers due to restrictions regarding distancing and hours of operation. That hurts manufacturers, distributors, shop owners, and the part-time employees, who have no other form of income. A significant percentage of employees have lost their jobs, 15 as businesses shut down temporarily or long term. This has hit part-timer workers including students supporting themselves through school. Without this income, students have struggled to pay rent and buy daily necessities.

●NOTES●

3 **altruism**「利他主義」他人の幸福や利益を第一の目的にする考え方 (⇔egoism)／8 **scarlet fever**「猩紅 (しょうこう) 熱」／9 **Zoom**　オンライン上でセミナーやミーティングを開催できる Web 会議システム／9 **FaceTime**　Apple 社製品同士をつなぐビデオ通話アプリ／12 **businesses**「商売、事業」

✻ *Comprehension Check* ✻

3. Appreciation of public health and medical staff members . . .

    a. has increased during the pandemic.

    b. has declined due to lack of support.

    c. is limited to the government.

4. Which of the following is NOT true?

    a. We appreciate opportunities to spend time with other people.

    b. During previous pandemics there were no ways to communicate with others.

    c. Some employees have lost their jobs as businesses shut down.

For full-time workers, there is a new work style. For the majority, this entails at least some remote work. Being free from managers' supervision and interruptions has been a pleasant change for some workers. But some miss the casual conversation with coworkers at the office and during lunch breaks.

We need to think not about "post-Covid" but "with Covid," because virus variants will continue to appear. Even if everyone is fully vaccinated and there are timely boosters, we need to focus on a creating a "new normal." Although we may long for a "return" to previous routines, the wiser path—like those that followed earlier pandemics—is to see this break in past routines as an opportunity to do things in new ways of doing things.

Liberation from the old routines could stimulate new opportunities to discover what is really important in life and allow us the option of trying to do things in new ways. The pandemic has greatly affected college education. The face-to-face contact between professors and students and between classmates has long been considered essential to the learning process. We have assumed that learning is dependent on lectures and seminars, on questions and answers exchanged in the same room. This may be a time to consider new approaches to learning.

●NOTES●
5 **virus variants**「ウイルスの変異体」 ／ 7 **boosters**「(免疫効果増進のための) 追加の予防接種」

✱ Comprehension Check ✱

5. Once everyone is vaccinated and receives boosters . . .
   a. college education will return to the previous routine.
   b. workers will all return to the workplaces as they used to do.
   c. we should consider finding new ways of working and learning.

❀ Structure Practice ❀

A. Choose the one underlined word or phrase that should be corrected or rewritten. Then change it so the sentence is correct.

1. ₁<u>Attempt</u> to prevent the spread of epidemics have been ₂<u>obstructed</u> by the ₃<u>movement</u> of people, animals, and ₄<u>viruses</u> across the globe.   [   ]

2. ₁<u>Release</u> from personal and ₂<u>society</u> routines has the ₃<u>potential</u> for ₄<u>stimulating</u> new ways of living, working, and even enjoying free time.   [   ]

B. Choose the word that best completes the sentence.

3. Due to the decrease of face-to-face encounters, we have to find new ways of reaching . . . to other people.
   a. about   b. around   c. forward   d. out

4. Everyone is hoping there will be a new medical . . . that will prevent further variants from appearing.
   a. breakoff   b. breakout
   c. breakthrough   d. breakup

5. Infection is . . . the transmission of the virus by molecules in the air, especially through sneezing, coughing, and speaking without a mask cover.
   a. affected by   b. due to   c. focused on   d. result from

❀ Listening Challenge ❀

🎧 **Listen and fill in the missing words.**
60

1. Despite [   ], epidemic diseases continue to develop because virus variants develop faster than human efforts to [

   ].

Life during a Pandemic   89

2. Once the bubonic plague [   ], towns and villages [
        ] and refused to allow travelers [   ].

3. [   ] municipal and national boundaries is [
        ] the chances that a new virus [
    ] new groups of people.

4. Having [   ] a lethargic state, she [   ]
    joining her friends in karaoke or going out to play tennis [   ].

5. Off [   ] a drone flying over rice fields, and then
    noticed that [   ] was using it to check the
    development of [   ].

Going Further (for discussion or research)

1. What strategies can you think of for overcoming what is called Corona fatigue?

2. How have you changed your life style during the pandemic?

3. What do you do when you want to relax?

Considering Tomorrow:
15 Changes to Prepare for
変わりゆく世界：明日の世界を考える15のトピック

編著者	James M. Vardaman
	野 地 薫
発行者	山 口 隆 史

発 行 所　　　株式会社 音羽書房鶴見書店

〒113-0033　東京都文京区本郷 3-26-13
TEL 03-3814-0491
FAX 03-3814-9250
URL: http://www.otowatsurumi.com
e-mail: info@otowatsurumi.com

2022 年 3 月 1 日　初版発行
2022 年 10 月 1 日　2 刷発行

組版・装幀　ほんのしろ
印刷・製本　（株）シナノ